I Beat the System!

William C. Brooks

ISBN 0-9705721-1-5

Printed in the United States of America

Dedication

To my wife and best friend, Elizabeth, the love of my life.

Table of Contents

1

It Takes a Village/1

2

Making a Difference/7

Race and the Military

3

Laboring/27

4

GM: A New Way of Seeing/60

5

How to Beat the System/70

A Message to Young Adults

Chapter One

It Takes a Village

In many ways I have followed in my father's footsteps.

He had big shoes. Born in 1889 in Missouri, he started working at the age of 14 for Civil War veteran and leading regional historian Gustavus St. Gemme. Four years later, in 1907, he started working for banker Henry L. Rozier, Sr., a loving association that lasted nearly 80 years until his death in 1984. He did odd jobs, but he also helped raise the Rozier children and was considered a part of the family.

Dad was an honored and decorated World War I veteran, and served in France at Argonne Forest, Chateau Thiery, and Catigny, Reims and Mets, some of the heaviest combat areas. He married my mother in 1928–she was a beloved educator, the first African-American from Ste. Genevieve to earn a college degree. In fact, during a time prior to desegregation, in 1941 she was elected vice-president of the Missouri Parent Teachers Association. She was a professor at Stowe Teachers College (now Harris-Stowe University in St. Louis). She was a consummate mother and professional, a woman who instilled in us the importance of knowing our history as African Americans. She made me play the violin–back then, there was no such thing as leaving those kinds of decisions to children!

My father fully partnered with my mother in the raising of their three sons: myself and two other brothers. When she died tragically in a car accident in 1942 at the age of 37, he was left to raise an 8-, 6- and 5-year old by himself. But he did it with grace, a clean conscience, and a spotless reputation–a legacy that all three of us strive to continue.

My father's legacy still lives. As a result of his associations and the respect he earned in the small community of Ste. Genevieve, Missouri, he has been honored with a street named after him. He found and purchased a home in 1924, something he was determined to do before he got married. He paid $1,800. for the wood frame house built between 1850 and 1880.

The house has a rich history. In 1854, a man by the name of Antoine LaGrave sued the local school system and won the house in the settlement. He and his wife Mary promptly sold the house to "Cassimere, a free man of color" for $30. Forty-two years later, Etienne Cassimere sold the place to Etienne Robinson for $10. The house was given in estate to Josephine Robinson, the daughter-in-law of Etienne. My father ultimately purchased the house from John and Josephine Robinson's heirs.

The home that we grew up in is located on Ste. Genevieve's west end, an area known as "Mudtown." The residents in the neighborhood were predominantly white, and my parents were somehow able to purchase a home and move in without incident. We were one of only two or three African American families in the area, and we played freely and without parental objection with the white children. It was here that my life and perspectives were shaped. I learned early in life that white people were neither to be obsessively revered nor feared. I value those times.

In 2000, the "Historic Brooks House," as it came to be called, was nominated by the Ste. Genevieve Landmarks Commission as one of Missouri's most endangered places. The Missouri Alliance for Historic Preservation, understanding the worth of the house as an important relic that recalled the black presence in French colonial Ste. Genevieve, agreed, and the momentum was set to begin renovation work. The plan is to turn the house into a museum that highlights and chronicles the role of blacks in this small Missouri community.

Ste. Genevieve, as all other towns and cities in the '20s, was segregated educationally. My brothers and I all graduated 8th grade from a one-room schoolhouse where my parents had both attended: Lincoln Elementary School. Our father was determined for us to attend high school, and both local high schools were for whites only. So he made the determination to ship us out. I attended St. Joseph's High School in St. Louis, Missouri and lived with relatives. I would never permanently return to Ste. Genevieve.

St. Louis was a completely new experience for me. I had never been to a movie, eaten at a restaurant or stayed at a hotel. I stayed with my father's brother, Garfield and his wife, Aunt Teresa, who lived about twenty miles from the high school. Uncle Garfield was an entrepreneur who had part ownership in a restaurant and in a coal and wood business. They agreed to enroll me in the all-Black Catholic school. I loved the big city, and ventured both to the cinema and to my first restaurant. I ended up number one in my freshman class.

That would be short lived. By my sophomore year, I was playing football and starting to notice girls. My grades reflected the results of my inattention to academics. A young nun, a new schoolteacher named Sister Walter Marie, promptly pulled me off the team. It proved an excellent motivator, and I quickly got my act together and pulled my grades up enough to once again participate in football. We played Valle High School in Ste. Genevieve that year, the school that I had been unable to attend because of my color. We beat them soundly.

When I was 15, St. Louis integrated the city's public pools. Excited about this chance to swim in a pool that was clean and well-maintained, my group of friends and I took a trip to Fairgrounds Park and jumped in. Having played with whites my entire life up to that point, I was unprepared for the response.

They scrambled out of the water and started throwing bricks.

That one incident actually prompted a five-day race war in St. Louis. Maybe "war" is too extreme a word. It was a time of looting and skirmishes between blacks and whites; a few arrests were made, and the policing was fairly evenhanded racially. After the five days, the event was largely forgotten.

I then moved to live with a cousin and her husband in St. Louis, to be closer to school. Another cousin in the area owned a chain of drug stores–remember, this was during a time when segregation virtually forced Blacks to form their own businesses and educational institutions–and I was able once again to work and earn my keep. I made the All-Catholic football and basketball teams for St. Louis, and managed to keep up with the books.

The St. Louis neighborhood of my teen years was quite different from my days at St. Genevieve. It was a rough, all-Black neighborhood, complete with gangs and territories. But it provided another place for me to refine what would turn out to be some very important social skills. As it turned out, I lived in one "territory," went to school in another, and worked for the drug store in yet another turf area. I had to become familiar and conversant with each area and with each set of communities. As it turned out, my reputation as an athlete helped. I was able to navigate without conflict in each neighborhood; living in one, working in another, and attending school in a third–all in the course of a day! I came to be known, and counted even some of the gang members among my friends and acquaintances. That, plus the years spent in all-white St. Genevieve, prepared me well for my later experiences in the military, General Motors, government service, and entrepreneurship.

In my later teen years, I considered the priesthood, something that Sister Walter Marie had intended for me. But when a friend tried that route and came back to tell me about it, I changed my mind. It seemed that the life of a priest was pretty isolated and I decided I would not take well to such confinement. Upon graduation from high school, I took a job as an office clerk at Olian Advertising in St. Louis. Shortly after, I joined the United States Air Force.

But I never lost touch with Sister Walter Marie. We corresponded at least twice a year, and she and my father became good friends. She invested time and care in me, and she wanted to make sure that I stayed on the right path. In addition to my father, mother, and extended family, I give her credit as a partner in my success.

I enlisted in the U.S. Air Force in November of 1951 and attended Basic Training at Lackland Air Force Base in San Antonio, Texas. Even though I had experienced segregated schools in Missouri, I was unprepared to be ordered to the back of the bus in San Antonio. Whites and blacks got along pretty well in my hometown, and I had traveled public transportation in St. Louis without incident. This was definitely a new experience.

Like my father, I got assigned to France in Laon, a city just outside of Paris, where I served for three years. I ran track, participated in the ceremony of coronation of Queen Elizabeth, and met many of the African American celebrities of the day–from Sugar Ray Robinson to Sidney Bechet and all the Black jazz musicians, for whom Paris was a welcome respite from American racism.

After returning to Vance Air Force Base in Enid, Oklahoma in June 1955, I reenlisted, was transferred to Mitchell Air Force Base in Hempstead, New York, and married Elizabeth Walters in 1956. Our marriage continues to be one of the joys of my life—one of the best things I ever did!

Recalling the high priority my parents gave to education, I completed a Bachelor of Arts Degree in Economics from Long Island University in New York, then a Masters in Business Administration from the University of Oklahoma in 1966, where I was stationed at the time. I was the first black person to receive the MBA degree from the university there.

My degrees gave me plenty of opportunities within the service. I worked at the Pentagon, building mathematical models of the workforce as a Systems Analyst and Econometrician. After a stint as Chief of the Personnel Data Systems Division in Bolling Air Force Base in Washington, D.C., I was assigned the job of Community Relations Specialist for the Job Corps within the U.S. Department of Labor.

The Job Corps position, I came to believe, was tailor-made to prepare me for one of my most memorable experiences. After working to set up Job Corps offices around the country, I was assigned to the Department of Defense staff to help address racial problems in the military. That position and that experience would take me down a completely new path–one I would never have imagined.

Chapter Two

Making a Difference: Race and the Military

The U.S. Armed Forces has always had a somewhat unique position in the race relations struggle here in the United States. First, all soldiers were bound by necessity because of a common goal that was repeated almost daily: to defend the country against aggressors and possible aggressors. That created a dynamic that altered the nature of the racial struggle within the military.

During World War II, the White House tried to adjust the conflicting demands of the civil rights leaders and the Army traditionalists. A certain amount of racial integration was inevitable during a war that mobilized a biracial army of eight million men. Through administrative error or necessity, the understood rule of segregation was ignored on many occasions, and black and white soldiers often worked and lived together in hospitals, rest camps, schools, and, more rarely, units. But these were isolated cases, touching relatively few men, and they had no recognizable effect on racial policy.

World War II, though, marked the beginning of an important step in the evolution of the civil rights movement. Until then the struggle for racial equality had been sustained chiefly by the "talented tenth," the educated, middle-class black citizens who formed an economic and political alliance with white supporters. The efforts of men like W. E. B. DuBois, Walter White, Thurgood Marshall of the NAACP and Lester Granger of the National Urban League were in the mainstream of the American reform movement, which stressed nonviolent social change and an orderly petitioning of government for a redress of grievances.

The growing political power of the Negro (the term in use at the time) and the threat of mass action in the 1940's were important reasons for the breakthrough on the color front that began in the armed forces in the postwar period. For despite the measure of good will and political acumen that characterized his social programs, Harry S. Truman might never have made the effort to achieve racial equality in the services without the constant pressure of civil rights activists. Here is a short history of that period:

Race Relations in the Armed Forces, 1945-1950

1945-46

A Board is established by Secretary of War Robert Patterson to address African Americans in the military. Named after its Chairman, General Alvan C. Gillem, Jr., this "Gillem Board" issues a report entitled "Utilization of Negro Manpower in the Postwar Army Policy." The report concludes that the Army's future policy should be to eliminate all special race-based treatment–but, curiously, does not question the continuing practice of racial segregation. In the meantime, the state of Georgia witnesses the brutal murder of two African American veterans and their wives. President Truman instructs the Justice Department to investigate this and similar crimes of oppression. He writes a letter to the National Urban League obligating the U.S. government to protect all citizens' civil rights, and appoints the President's Committee on Civil Rights as part of that commitment.

1947-48

The President's Committee on Civil Rights issues its landmark report condemning and urging an immediate end to discrimination and segregation in the armed forces. Civil rights activists A.

Philip Randolph and Grant Reynolds organize the Committee Against Jim Crow in Military Service and Training. Truman issues Executive Order 9981: "It is hereby declared to be the policy of the President that there shall be equality of treatment and opportunity for all persons in the armed services without regard to race, color, religion, or national origin." The order also establishes the President's Committee on Equality of Treatment and Opportunity in the Armed Services. After disgruntled army officers question whether segregation is officially banned, Truman states in a press conference that the intent of Executive Order 9981 is to end segregation in the armed forces. The army experiments with integrated units, and nudges slowly towards merit assignments and promotions for African Americans.

1949-50

The resistance within military leadership continues, with the President insisting on movement and the leadership defending its various discriminatory policies. At the time, only one of 8,200 Marine officers is African American and only five of the Navy's 45,000 officers are African American. The U.S. Army submits an integration plan that limits the number of African American recruits to 10% to keep their numbers down; they ultimately abandon the quota aspect of the plan.

Fast forward to 1971. Segregation in the armed forces had been outlawed by Executive Order by President Harry Truman more than 20 years ago. Despite those steps, the justice wheels still turned slowly, and it was no better in the U.S. military.

In May of 1971, we experienced the largest ever outbreak of racial violence in Air Force history. More than 200 airmen brawled over a three-day period. Fights during that time resulted in serious injuries, even deaths. We were wasting energy fighting each other instead of the enemy. After that, black airmen began to air their grievances, ranging from discrimination in assignments to lack of recreational facilities.

I was a Captain at the time, and I saw it up close. I knew the game: there was a clear correlation between promotion and graded performance. Blacks and whites who received similar scores were given similar opportunities to advance. But blacks were never graded as highly as whites were, even when their performance was up to par. We would "just miss" getting that promotion, "just miss" a better-than-average rating. On paper, everything looked fair and equitable. But I knew differently.

Finally I got my chance to speak up. I had been on loan from the Air Force to work with the Job Corps, and the military superiors knew of the progress we made there. They decided to study the issue of race relations in the military.

Senator Edward Kennedy advanced the issue in the Congress in a series of hearings on race relations in the military. Were Black officers promoted as fast as white officers? Once he asked the question, the military brass knew it had to respond. They came to ask me for help.

My response was to tell them what I knew. I provided all the statistical evidence that was needed to back up my claim. The statistics had always been there; but the conclusion had never publicly or officially been drawn: that gradings and promotions were completely equitable on paper, but blacks hardly ever seemed to "make the grade."

The disturbing result? In-fighting. Blacks and whites fought each other as much as they did the enemy. The Vietnam War was in full swing, and, as everyone who studies American history now knows, we were not winning. The top brass recognized that this had to be a hindrance to our military progress. Air Force Major General Lucius Theus, an African American, was appointed to lead a study on this critical issue.

Something very interesting was going on at the time in Canada. They seemed to have the same kind of issue. But in this case, it was French-speaking officers vs. English-speaking officers. The English-speaking officers always seemed to get the promotions. It was a clear case of discrimination.

Their response was...novel? Not exactly. This kind of practice has been around for years. The United States had even ventured into this area, with special consideration given to the WWII veterans with the G.I. Bill that provided low-interest housing loans and subsidies for college costs. And of course we all know about the preferences given to persons merely by virtue of wealth or status, although those "perks" were never codified.

It was, however, something that organizations had rarely done quite as explicitly as this. The Canadian military simply gave the French-speaking officers extra "points," simply by virtue of their language status. What a concept!

I ended up recommending the same for our African American military personnel. But I knew that alone would not solve our military's racial problems.

I knew that whites were not all bad. I knew it from my years of interacting with them, as a child, as a student, as a professional. I had seen the gamut of personality, the gamut of political and social views, the gamut of racist and non-racist attitudes and values. This one thing I believed: any effort to address race in the military was going to take education, education on a massive scale.

Defense Secretary Melvin Laird named a group of us–Colonel Al Kilby, Colonel Ed Krise, and myself–to a Task Force that would, according to an agenda-setting memorandum, "develop a program to foster understanding between the majority and minority ethnic groups with a resultant improvement in racial attributes and beliefs." The Task Force was formed to consider how to implement the recommendations suggested in the "Theus Study" on race and the military. I was proud to be part of a military group named for an African American man who was greatly admired by many, including myself.

The Task Force's main recommendation was to open an institute for all U.S. Armed Forces members. The program would be mandatory for all active duty military personnel. The officers–the military's leaders–would have to go through the training first; they would then take lower-ranking personnel through the program. A Race Relations Education Board made up of representatives from the Office of Secretary of Defense's educational and civil rights areas would oversee the effort and provide policy direction. The people they placed on this Board would prove to be very important.

The brass called me back from my Job Corps assignment, along with Colonel Al Kilby (black) and Colonel Ed Krise (white), to implement the study's recommendations. I could envision a real educational effort where we addressed gut-level issues and really made headway in the races understanding each other. As we began our discussions, neither I nor my colleagues pulled any punches. I, for one, wanted the commanding officers to know that every single black military person felt the sting of racism. I wanted them to understand the effect it had on the effectiveness of the armed forces overall. I wanted them to see the urgency of the problem, and agree that we needed to put serious resources into addressing it.

The proposal called for an intensive training effort. There would be testing. There would be lectures. There would be discussion. There would even be field trips. It would get lively. We would clue our white counterparts in on aspects of the black experience they knew nothing about. We would dig. We would challenge. We would inform. We would be provocative. And all of it would be necessary.

Needless to say, there was opposition. We wrestled about the particulars. I felt it wasn't going fast enough. We weren't getting anything done. So I pulled out a long-standing strategy of public sector personnel: I leaked word of our stalemate to the press. Once the press made it an issue, the military "higher-ups" made it a priority.

Guerilla warfare is not just for war between countries. We as African Americans had to learn early that out-thinking the opponent with strategy would work a lot better than overt protest, which is easy to shoot down. The press leak was just one example of non-violent "guerilla warfare."

Senator Robert Byrd was one definitely not on our side. He accused us of trying to 'brainwash' people. Our response was that we were trying to impact behavior, not attitudes. What you think of me is not my business. We simply wanted people to engage in righteous behaviors. We wanted officers to be treated fairly in objectively measurable ways. We wanted equity codified and its laws adhered to. We took the concept of "law and order" and simply applied it to discrimination and racism.

Our proposal had a component devoted to racial understanding, certainly. We knew that understanding would help. But our emphasis was on helping officers understand what behaviors were expected, and what would and would not be tolerated.

The plan was to avoid a formal and sterile class environment in order to elicit genuine interaction and understanding among the military's diverse groups. We did not limit our curriculum to the mere conveying of information. Instructors were trained to adapt the discussion groups (or to use a euphemism, "rap sessions") to the individuals involved. They were taught to use filmed "case studies" to invite feedback and discussion and provoke thought.

In addition to Robert Byrd's predictable resistance, we had sophisticated enemies at the highest levels. But we also had a high-level person who supported our efforts: the Assistant Secretary of Defense for Manpower. He worked directly for Melvin Laird. "We're fighting a war; we don't have time for that (racial infighting)," he would say to me. He clearly understood priorities, and was very matter-of-fact and pragmatic. Practical people tend not to have the particularly virulent strains of racism that inflict those with more intolerant views. The Deputy Assistant Secretary of Defense, Don Miller (now a successful businessman and former Vice-President of Consolidated Edison), supported us as well.

Those in the military understand the concept of "cover." In the heat of battle, those going out into an open and vulnerable place need to be "covered" by their partners behind the lines. Their fellow fighters attack from a hidden place so that they can charge the enemy. We who were starting this strategy of racial education–a radical strategy for its time–needed plenty of "cover" if we were to be successful. I am grateful that we had that. The idea would have been dead in the water otherwise.

To my surprise, Secretary Laird bought the entire package. So we began. We found that in the planning process, rank was no longer relevant. I was the one with the most passion of the three, so I got picked to be the "talking head."

I remember my first presentation to explain the concept to top military brass. The Assistant Secretary was there, as well as

Deputy Assistant Don Miller, Navy Chairman Admiral E.R. Zumwalt, Jr. and a Three-Star General.

The General was not impressed. In fact, he threatened me. “Captain,” he said, “I’ll promote you so fast I’ll destroy you.” This is the kind of sophisticated opposition we were up against. The General knew better than to argue us on our ideas. He was going to take the back way, appearing supportive at the same time he was stabbing me–and the effort–in the back.

We had opposition from surprising corners. The Assistant Secretary of the Navy was black, and attended the presentation. His response made my hair stand up: “Not everyone needs help, Bill. My own son is well-educated; I’m not looking for a handout for him.” I looked him dead on, eye to eye. I didn’t even take a breath. “Mr. Secretary, at the end of the day, your son is still a nigger.”

All blacks understood this. Some just didn’t want to acknowledge it.

I *knew* I was fired. But my fellow fighters covered for me. Not only blacks but white officers and officials too. “Bill, you have to understand,” said the Assistant Secretary. “He’s not very black.”

I understood.

After that, things began to move, and quickly. Krise was named Head of the newly named Defense Race Relations Institute, or DRRI. I was Chief of Ethnic Studies, and Kilby was a Deputy Director. Our first task was to decide on a place. Mississippi was too volatile, so we settled on Patrick Air Force Base in Cocoa Beach, Florida.

Finally, we had a pilot program. It was conducted by the Assistant Secretary of Defense in October, 1970. From that pilot, we refined the curriculum and established our instructors. One month later, on November 1, 1970, we conducted our first Institute class with ten Army, ten Navy, and twelve Air Force officers. The Air Force team stayed an additional week to critique the class; and to get additional training to allow them to serve as monitors for other classes. Each team then conducted pilot programs at their own respective bases (Ellsworth and Lackland in Texas, Davis Monthan in Arizona, Travis in California, Chanute in Illinois, and Patrick in Cocoa Beach, Florida). Those programs were similarly evaluated by the permanent DRRI faculty members or the Air Force staff monitors.

The name of the game was evaluate, evaluate, evaluate. In this new and radical concept, there was no room for error. Everyone had to be on board. Our evaluators even came to see themselves as "owners" of the effort. They became our most ardent supporters even as they provided excellent critique.

We learned a lot in that test operation. First, we knew that the instructors we chose would have to be well-trained and experienced in all aspects of race relations. We ended up requiring that all instructors also be DRRI graduates. Secondly, we knew that the curriculum needed much work.

We developed an extensive 6-week curriculum: 77 hours of Ethnic Studies; 46 hours of Social Sciences related to race relations) 48 hours of Community Interaction; and a 70-hour Practicum in Group Leadership. We appointed students to serve as discussion leaders for the ethnic studies and social science instruction. The group leadership module emphasized the dynamics of leading this kind of course, complete with practice sessions, instruction in how to prevent polarization between groups and individuals, and some general information on Department of Defense goals, policies, and directives. This would allow our instructors to read from the same page and have credibility with the students when leading discussions.

I would generally start the sessions with a speech. I knew the first question on everyone's lips: "Why do we even need this?" They rarely would ask the question outright, but their faces, their body language, told me what was in their hearts. Here was my answer:

Why Is The Defense Race Relations Institute Needed?
by William C. Brooks

"Segregation and discrimination in the military services were officially ended by President Truman in 1948. We all realize that attitudes and habitual ways of looking at things don't change because of new rules and regulations. While discrimination was officially wiped off of the books 23 years ago, racial unrest exists in the military today as it did then.

"Divisiveness and racial polarity have surfaced in our system and are approaching the self-destruct level. We will not be able to defend our nation or support national policy if this turmoil continues. We can't let the race issue divide and weaken us.

"The Department of Defense has the most equitable policy for equal opportunity of any agency within the government. But they are only policies until they are converted into action.

"Each of us brings to our service life a part of our home culture. When we return to civilian life, a lot of service experience goes with us. We can see that the problems of the military are identical to the problems of the civilian community.

"Education is one of the keys to solving the problem of racial polarity. Can we look at our black servicemen and relate them to the glorious American heritage? What about Chicano Americans? Do we know about American Indians who fought for the United States? *If we haven't done at least some reading in these areas, we are not living up to our responsibilities as military leaders.*

"One of the most criticized aspects of military life has to do with social activities. This is probably the area of conflict which causes most of the emotional problems.

"The challenge, as I see it, is to meet the problem head on. We must not be hesitant about communicating with each other on these mutual problems.

"Do commanders have racial problems? They do and admit it now. A year ago they would probably have said, "nothing goes on here that we can't handle." The dramatic shift from confidence to confession has come about because a number of racial incidents reached tragic proportions during the last year. The armed forces battled these racial outbreaks as they occurred; but, as military tradition would have it, there was a general reluctance to admit that a racial problem existed. After all, the argument went, the uniformed services have been in the vanguard of integration since 1948. It was the consensus among military men that integration in the armed forces was working well. True equality was possible in the military profession, or so the story went.

"The mounting numbers of racial brawls during the past two years is distressing. Because minority fighting men have proven their courage in combat – one-fifth of the Medal of Honor Awards in Vietnam have gone to Blacks. For decades, white officers and NCOs (Non-Commissioned Officers) have proudly stated that only a man's performance mattered, not the color of his skin. Everyone was equal. Assignments, promotions, housing, privileges and punishments were to be meted out without racial discrimination. Any proven instances of discrimination were to be dealt with promptly and objectively. Thus, there would be no problems in any of the services based on race, color or creed. The white man in uniform believed this. The black man did not; he does not today. While actions were taken at DOD level to counter the growing unrest among black military personnel, they were largely superficial, although some substantial improvements have occurred.

"The rise of Black militancy in civilian life, fired by the death of Martin Luther King and the rising eloquence of such Black spokesmen as Malcolm X, Stokely Carmichael, Eldridge Cleaver and H. Rap Brown, began to affect the attitudes of Black men coming into the military. They became more vocal in expressing their complaints about real or imagined discrimination, and the rhetoric of the Black militants is heard more frequently in the barracks. Although combat duty in Vietnam tended to solidify the races, Blacks and whites went their separate ways for off-duty recreation. Friendships, fostered by the strains of war, disintegrated when troops returned to the states. This meant nothing to the whites; but, to the blacks, it meant that there had been no change in the basic anti-black attitude of the white majority while they had been laying their lives on the line.

"Commanders have used black officers and NCOs out of the chain of command to dispose of problems involving black servicemen. This action is resented by black servicemen. It is interpreted as a fear or reluctance on the part of white leaders to get involved in any discussion with racial overtones.

"Today's black serviceman is different from his counterpart of ten years ago. Formerly, he countered acts of racial discrimination only with hard work and endurance. Today he is more likely to make his resentment known. Today, in the young black soldier, there often is more personal and racial pride, more bitterness at real or imagined injustice.

"Minority members need to sense whether a commander can treat a complaint of racial discrimination calmly and objectively. He needs a commander who recognizes such slogans as "Black is Beautiful," as a mere gesture of pride, comradeship and solidarity. The commander must understand his men before he writes off the spirited ones, who may be potential leaders, as troublemakers or militants. On the other hand, he must be firm and ensure that his troops realize that discipline is not discrimination. If minority troops feel an alienation, it usually springs from resentment at society in general – at the imperfections in the country that they are defending with their lives.

"We have all read or heard a great deal about black militancy and no doubt found it difficult to understand militant blacks or how to relate to them. If you were to ask me how one should deal with militant blacks, I could only answer: all black Americans are militant, angry and hostile. To talk about the black militant is to talk about all of us. We might show it in different ways, express it in different language or behavioral styles, but black militancy it is and it is important that we all understand this. In today's society, the young black militant is resolved to destroy institutional racism and every vestige of second-class citizenship and he is carrying this militancy into the armed services.

"Minority service members seem to have lost faith in the military system. They are not aware of the many accomplishments of the Department of Defense in their behalf, and our leaders are either unaware that their troops have complaints or are unpre-

> pared to handle the problems which come to their attention. Leaders avoid talking about a war which is fought every night in the barracks and other places where servicemen gather. Report after report continues to drive home the message that our principal problem is that people don't communicate. With racial discord as the greatest morale problem, and the most difficult challenge to leadership today, the services nevertheless continue to turn loose its officers and NCOs to muddle through these problems with little formal training. A need clearly exists for instruction on race relations to sensitize our leaders and give them the assistance they urgently need. Although the roots of the race problem lie outside the military, the tendrils have spread within it. They must be recognized and dealt with. Gentlemen, the Defense Race Relations Institute is the vehicle by which the needed massive doses of education in race relations can be delivered to all of our fellow service members.
>
> "By the nature of Travis, LeJuene, Frankfurt, Quantico, Ft. Ord, Turkey, Okinawa, [various military bases], it seems gentlemen that we are engaged in a revolution and this is our last chance to become aware and make it a peaceful revolution. We challenge you gentlemen to absorb this training here – and return to your bases, posts and ships to replace racial unrest with racial harmony."

By now, things were getting pretty dicey. Publicity was growing, and I seemed to be the one chosen to respond to the press. Then, I started getting calls whenever a base was experiencing race problems. I developed a reputation. Seeing me in action with my dashiki and afro, certain circles began calling me "Captain Blood." The Brotherhood Association of Military Airmen, an African American group, had coined the name for me, and it stuck. I didn't disappoint. I invited–and got–Rev. Jesse Jackson, Dick Gregory, even Nikki Giovanni to read her controversial poetry. I had no problem acting like a bulldozer, if that's what was needed. I found myself in a role of "link." I served as a point of access for black soldiers who felt left out of the system. They used me to access the hierarchy, and I didn't hesitate to make their concerns and views known.

Then, a happy surprise. I got more cover. Assistant Secretary Miller hired Captain Curtis Smothers, an African American attorney, to work as his Deputy. He was a savvy attorney, and helped cover for me when I really made the army folks angry.

I became known for not backing down on anything. One of our presentations was to the Assistant Secretary. Colonel White criticized me on my appearance after the presentation: "Captain, you need a haircut."

"I'm not getting a haircut 'til you get some black barbers in here!" was my reply. I wanted them to know that no issue was too small–at least as long as the racism was so rampant and thick.

Don Miller was getting antsy with me. "Bill, you're raising too much hell." I didn't care. He kept trying to tone me down, and I kept refusing.

It finally got to be too much. Colonel White and Colonel Krise went to D.C. to meet with Miller. It seemed they wanted to fire me for insubordination. Miller called to let me know. He warned me of their actions. "Bill, I didn't buy it. I told them I wouldn't allow you to be fired. But now they want to move you to Europe." (Remember "I'll promote you so fast I'll destroy you"? This was the strategy. It might have worked.) He continued, "Bill don't go to Europe, whatever you do. Stay there–but cool out."

One week later, Krise called a staff meeting. He was visibly collected, but I knew he was shaken. "I have been relieved of my command." Turns out Miller fired him, and replaced him with an African American, Colonel Claude Dixon. Of course, certain people did not want that to happen. The number one and two positions in the Institute held by blacks? For some, that simply would not be.

I think that's why I got a call during a party I was hosting for some of the officers. "Dixon's been arrested and charged with rape." The alleged victim was a white woman.

Dixon was found not guilty. But he was transferred to a military base in Alabama. His replacement was also African American, but more of a team player, more likely to toe the line.

Nevertheless, we continued with the classes. We took one of our first group of "students" from the isolated Patrick Air Force Base to Miami–that was what we formally called "Community Interaction." We wanted the officers of the lighter persuasion to see some of the grittiness we had seen. We took them to stay in hotels frequented by Blacks, we took them to bars in Black neighborhoods, we exposed them to street life. We even visited local jails. Nobody wore their stripes. In this group, unlike the rest of the armed services, everyone had equal status.

Then, we showed still another side: the Black church. An eye-opening experience for those who were used to no church at all, or to a more solemn and somber worship experience. We visited the Hispanic community, too, as well as low-income Anglo communities.

After this kind of whirlwind exposure, we took our group, heads still spinning, to Palm Beach. We wanted them to see the contrast up close, in a way that could not be denied.

Interestingly enough, we had to learn diversity just as the students did. When we found out that the officers who hailed from Appalachia would simply not drink cold beer, we had to respect that–as we learned that multicultural teaching was a two-way street.

As we modeled that respect, we found that the results of our first training class were nothing short of phenomenal. We saw whites "radicalized" in just a few short weeks. Even the General who had threatened to fire me had to admire the impact we were making. He went from "threatening" me with a promotion to saying, without hesitation and without embarrassment, "Captain, you're doing a hell of a job here!" For me that was affirmation, and a sign that the results were more than worth the risk.

And a side benefit: the training produced a kind of camaraderie, not just between Blacks and whites, but within Blacks of varying ranks. This kind of "fun", but serious, test, would help things along.

We had a tall goal: to promote change throughout the organization; to "beat the system." We wanted to improve communications, decrease the violence among military personnel, and stop racist practices in their tracks.

Organizationally, we knew that the Institute would have to become part of the fabric of the military. The Equal Opportunity Officer would have to be involved to provide information and perspective. Perhaps the base Chaplain or psychiatrist would participate in the sessions or provide follow-up counseling and/or consultation. We spelled this out in the documentation, so that everyone knew what the vision was. We repeated this vision and structure to literally thousands of trainers. Many, black and white, had been indoctrinated for too long with the wrong message: one of mistrust, one of hate, miseducation at its finest. We knew that we would have to reverse the process. We indoctrinated them so that they would in turn indoctrinate others.

Some of the tools we used were heavy-handed, designed to really open eyes and raise consciousnesses. Others introduced some levity, like this one: a glossary of African American slang. See how many you already know. See how many are still in force today. See how many have been integrated into our nation's vernacular.

Ain't Coming - statement of refusal
Aunt Jane – female Uncle Tom
Baby – term of address for one's love or spouse but also a word used in general conversation, irrespective of the sexual identity or personal or social relationship.
Back-door Man – a married woman's lover, who is incidentally, a legendary figure in blues numbers
Bad – a simple reversal of the white standard, the very best
Bad Nigger – a black person who refuses to be meek or who rejects the social terms of poverty and oppression the culture designs for him
Bad Dogs – bad feet
Bag – one's disposition, mood, behavior, life-style, vocation, hobby, interests; a social milieu or clique
Big Apple – any big northern city but especially New York, term originated among widely traveled jazzmen
Black Bottom – the area where the "nitty-gritty" black population of any town or city resides.
Blood – one black person to another; wine.
Blow – the message of a person's conversation; what he said that particular time. Synonym: rap

Blow Your Mind – to get high on a hallucinogenic drug or an idea, or from seeing a good movie or painting or sunrise, etc.
Burn – to cook food or to cheat someone
Burner – the tops in his field
Changes, Going through some – having difficulties; regularly on the receiving end of bad news
Charlie – a corruption of "Mister Charlie," any white man; originally, the overseer or boss
Chill'lins 101 – derogatory phrase applied to any Black Studies course in U.S. schools
Cop a Plea – to be verbally evasive
Cracker – a white person. One theory holds that it's a term from the 19th century back-country of Georgia, coined by black people – a reference deriving from the whip-cracking slaveholder. Another theory is that it comes from the white soda cracker as opposed to, say, ginger cookies
Dap – impeccably attired. Synonym: clean
Dozens, Playing the – A contest to see which young brother can remember or make up the greatest number of obscene, rhymed couplets reflecting on the opponent's parents. Sometimes called "signifying" or "mamma talk." Sometimes done with fingersnapping accompaniment. Though it may start in fun, it often attracts a crowd of admirers and it can easily end in a fight. Not approved by parents.
Dust – to leave; money
Gig – a job. Synonyms: slave, hustle
Give (one) some slack – to show restraint; a plea for more sympathy and understanding
Grease – to eat
Grits – food in general
Hammer – beautiful Afro-American girl
Hard Leg – any man or an ugly woman
Heavy – an extremely intelligent person. But with a slight change in inflection, an extremely stupid person
Hit On – to make a request, especially for love-making
Member – an Afro-American, or Soul brother
Nose Wide Open – to be in love
Rep – reputation
Run it Down – to tell the whole truth of whatever is in question
Sky Up – to leave
Turf – the street one lives on
What It Is? – What's going on?

Things went along fairly well for a while. But occasionally we would get spurious comments–or spurious suggestions. Like the suggestion from Race Relations Institute Educational Advisor James Lovejoy, who wanted to include white ethnicity as an "integrated part of the Ethnic Studies Program." He wrote:

"The history, culture, immigrant status, etc. of white ethnic groups in America have conditioned them to act–and to react toward minority ethnic groups–in a particular way.

"More white ethnic groups still view minority groups, especially Blacks, as somehow inferior–intellectually, morally, socially, economically and politically–and they treat them accordingly wherever this is possible and advantageous to their own concern for power.

"However, there are a growing number of whites within those majority groups who are genuinely and actively concerned about the injustices and inequalities perpetuated against some Americans...

"To neglect or deny recognition of white contributions is as wrong as to gloss over the injustices perpetuated against minority groups by the majority...

"A question which might be considered in one of the classes is "Why do we have individual white liberals (or conservatives) espousing the cause of oppressed minorities while at the same time members of those same minorities, who have achieved economic and social status, will not take positions of leadership for their own people?"

"Both Whites and Blacks (along with other minority ethnic groups) must begin to deal with persons and not stereotypes or 'typical' or general categories, if there is to be any racial harmony and ultimate racial equality in America."

At first, I was angry. I had much to say to this gentleman, but I had to say it with tact and in a way that would teach and not berate. I had to let him know that "white ethnic" history had already been taught to the people we were trying to reach via the Race Relations Institute. It is the same ironic argument I hear whites sometimes make about Historically Black Colleges and Universities (HBCUs). "Why do they have to have their own universities? How would 'they' like it if we had separate universities?" They forget their history: these universities were started when 'they' wouldn't let 'us' in to their institutions, even when we were exceptionally qualified. Here was my response:

> "There is not time, nor is there sufficient reason or evidence to substantiate our dealing with this subject. Whites usually band together as whites, not Poles, Germans, English, Frenchmen, etc., against blacks and other non-white minorities and forget that they are an ethnic group. Whites, regardless of their ethnic group, have not been stripped of their history, cultural, status, etc., as have non-white minorities. We are filling in what history books have left out."

To add to the curriculum in this way, I continued, would dilute it. I pointed out that the curriculum does include the contributions of all Americans regardless of color in combating racism. I pointed out that his singling out of Blacks as being especially responsible for fighting discrimination was itself a form of stereotyping. Then, I invited him to develop a proposed curriculum for our consideration.

My last and parting phrase: "We are considering adding a block of instruction on "White Backlash." I trust he got the point.

I would say that all of us who were involved in this endeavor from the beginning would say that we are proud that the Institute still continues today. It is now called the "Defense Equal Opportunity Management Institute, or DEOMI, renamed in 1979 to reflect its widened scope that now addresses sexual harassment, sexism, extremism, religious accommodations and anti-Semitism. It boasts nearly 20,000 graduates from the active and reserve forces as well as the U.S. Coast Guard, and now features a comprehensive curriculum that includes courses in equal opportunity for advisors, officers and program managers; instruction in interpersonal relationships and issues; courses designed specifically for strategic, high-level decision makers; and specially designed research and internship programs. Most importantly, the Institute conducts periodic surveys to provide the most current information on the state of diversity within the military.

One survey in particular is designed to help commanders improve their equal opportunity and organizational climates. Only the commander can request the survey; only the commander can review the survey results. Since 1990, more than 6,000 unit-level surveys have been completed.

Surveys measure these 12 factors: 1) Sexual Harassment and (Sex) Discrimination; 2) Differential Command Behavior toward Minorities; 3) Positive Equal Opportunity Behaviors; 4) Racist/Sexist Behaviors; 5) "Reverse" Discrimination; 6) Organizational Commitment; 7) Perceived Work Group Effectiveness; 8) Job Satisfaction; 9) Discrimination against Minorities and Women; 10) "Reverse" Discrimination II; 11) Attitudes toward Racial Separatism; and 12) Overall Equal Opportunity (EO) Climate.

Interestingly, the Institute has also expanded its mission to consult throughout the Department of Defense as well as internationally. It has served the countries of Burundi and South Africa, the Ukraine; the United Kingdom; Canada, and Russia in their efforts to democratize and create humanitarian environments.

It was an honor to have been part of an effort that has allowed so many African Americans and women to advance on the basis of merit and merit alone. While all of our institutions can still improve, and improve greatly, we can be proud of the progress that has been made in the U.S. military–an institution that has given birth to the career successes of the likes of Secretary of State Colin Powell, retired Major General Lucius Theus, who ended up in Detroit with Allied-Signal, Colonel Ruth Lucas (Ret.), a professor and one of my mentors as one of the first African American female colonels in the Air Force–and Bill Brooks.

Chapter Three

Laboring

In 1978, I was honored and humbled to share the stage with Civil Rights First Lady Rosa Parks in Pittsburgh, Pennsylvania. We were both getting awards from the National Association of Negro Business and Professional Women's Clubs for our commitment to civil rights. She said something to me that I never forgot. "You know, Mr. Brooks, those corporation jobs belong to the people who struggled to make it possible. Make sure you always work to enable other Blacks to get where you are."

I got a Ph.D. in the freedom struggle that night. I was able to sit, not only with Rosa Parks, but with another giant award winner: Ms. Unita Blackwell, then-mayor of a small city in Mississippi. I stayed up nearly all night listening to her stories about historic freedom fighter Fannie Lou Hamer, whom Blackwell served as a personal assistant. The things those two great women shared with me have soaked my consciousness. I will always be grateful to them.

Ten years later, their words and the memory of their commitment sparked me to take a huge pay cut in order to take on a huge challenge: the Labor Department. I had gone from an Air Force career to a brief and fairly uneventful tour in the Nixon White House, then to General Motors, where I found myself ensconced in computers and data, but with excellent compensation to provide for my family. Then, after 17 years and multitude of assignments, I found myself back in government service, ensconced this time in an unwieldy bureaucracy.

Compassionate conservatism is not a new idea. The new era of Labor saw then-Labor Secretary Elizabeth Dole and I working overtime to find and fine violators of children, violators of women and minorities, violators of farm workers–even violators who were well-known as protectors and defenders of the "least of these" like the Salvation Army. But more on that later.

I was working at GM corporate headquarters, readying myself for a long golf weekend at Myrtle Beach, when I got the call.

I wasn't looking for the call, mind you. But this was from a power broker married to a power broker. A Cabinet Secretary in the Reagan and Bush Administrations married to a U.S. Senator. I had met her when I was working in the Nixon White House, but I didn't really know her.

"I know what I'm looking for," she said. "I have a profile of what I want, and everyone I talk to tells me, 'You'd better talk to Bill Brooks.' I've been named Labor Secretary, and I'd like for you to be my Assistant Secretary."

I had the nerve to say "no" at first. I was happy. I was making money. I wasn't looking for a pay cut. I felt I was making an impact at GM. I had no reason to leave.

But Elizabeth Dole is hard to say "no" to. Especially when she got her people to lean on me. People like Bob Dole ("Elizabeth needs you."). People like President George Herbert Walker Bush ("Elizabeth needs you.").

Then, the clincher. "Bill, give me a chance," she said. I agreed to be in D.C. the Friday before my golf trip.

She was *good*. "I can't leave," I told her. "I'm making money, got kids in college." She came back strong. "Bill, the President called me before Christmas. He said 'I need you.' Understand, Bob and I were ready to move out of Watergate and make some real money ourselves. But I just couldn't turn this down. It's an opportunity to make a difference."

Then, "I don't want anyone to work for me who hasn't taken a serious cut in pay just to be here. That's the kind of dedication this work will require. I need someone like you–someone who knows how to manage a massive organization, who knows how to lead, who's not afraid of big dollars. Bill, we can make a difference here–in child and farm labor laws, the problem with the glass ceiling. I know how passionate you are about enforcement. You are the person."

I told her I'd think about it. I did–over the golf course, a good place to reflect. Then at home with my family. They did it for me. "You can't turn this down," they said. "You can't complain about the system and then refuse to do this."

I called Elizabeth the next day, and said, "I do." The commitment I was making, to me, was just about as serious as getting married. Elizabeth likes to tell this story. "I knew I had him," she is fond of saying, "when I got him to cut his golf trip short. I knew I had a serious shot at him then."

When I came to Labor from GM, I had learned lessons. I had learned not to get bogged down in details before I had a chance to get a birds-eye view, a landscape look. To do that, I had to talk to the people. People in the trenches, people who do the work. They're the ones who know.

So I went to them. I let them know I wanted to make their jobs easier, not harder. I wanted to discover the best way to do things. What I discovered was that the Department of Labor (DOL) had come under increasing scrutiny and criticism. Congress, especially the Democrats, had begun to see Labor as an operation that simply was not working on behalf of the workers. Just one example: contractors could be cited by Labor officials for wage violations–that is, not paying the proper hourly wage for various kinds of union jobs.

An administrative law judge could make that determination, but the administration had to recover the wages and pay the offended party. If Labor failed to completely follow through, the offended workers had no recourse. They could not themselves take any action to collect the underpayment.

I also discovered that the laws were not being enforced adequately, and that child labor and migrant farm workers were the "hot button" issues of the day.

I had already begun to formulate ideas. I was starting to get excited about the prospects. But first, I had to be confirmed.

This would not be easy. I was a Republican nominee in a Democratic congressional environment. And the gatekeeper was none other than Senator Edward "Ted" Kennedy, Chair of the Labor and Human Resources Committee, the Committee before which I would have to appear before a vote on my nomination could go to the full Senate.

In fact, I had to pass through two gatekeepers: Senator Kennedy and Senator Howard Metzenbaum of Ohio, who served as Chairman of the Labor Subcommittee under Kennedy's Committee. They were concerned about enforcement especially, and about what they felt were inadequate staffing levels for DOL to properly monitor and prosecute employers who violated labor standards for safety, health, and wages. I made the requisite assurances that I would review their concerns about specific matters and look closely at DOL staffing to make sure we had enough people to do the job.

But I had to do something else. I had to agree not to pursue a certain case. It was a case involving the U.S. Air Force. Apparently, the Wright-Patterson Air Force Base in Dayton, Ohio was trying to reduce wages for certain of its employees based on a comparison with similar civilian jobs, from $5.50 to $4.50 an hour. At the time, the median household income was about $30,000.00 annually, and the poverty level for a family of four was about $12,000.00. Apparently the Air Force was pursuing many other requests for similar wage reductions, and that had aroused the ire of Senator Metzenbaum. He wrote in a question to me, "Do you think it is sound policy for the Department of Labor to expend resources in trying to reduce the wages of workers who already are at the poverty line?"

An administrative law judge had already given its decision in the Wright-Patterson case. It turned down the Air Force's request to lower wages there. I found out through the grapevine that Senator Metzenbaum wanted to make sure that I, as Assistant Labor Secretary, would not appeal that decision. My confirmation would depend on my assurances that I would not pursue such an action.

Publicly, this was not supposed to happen. Designates for Cabinet-level posts are not supposed to agree to take specific actions on specific cases. But Metzenbaum and Kennedy were formidable, and they were not afraid to wield their power.

I have learned and been taught over the years to pick my fights carefully. Did I argue that they had no right to insist on this? I already believed that there was no reason to appeal, but what about the principle?

I agreed in writing not to pursue an appeal of the case. I had to be clear and specific, not agreeing in a way that would allow my office to wiggle out later. I wrote, "After consulting with the Office of the Solicitor (that was the DOL office that handled legal cases), I am prepared to state that if I am confirmed as Assistant Secretary we will not pursue an appeal of that decision."

I also agreed in that letter to narrow the wage gap between civilian and non-civilian employees, and to work quickly to publish new regulations on employment of disabled workers. These regulations had been slow in the making, but had cleared the final hurdle: approval by the Office of Management and Budget.

But regulations cannot be enforced until they are published. Shrewd administrators can hold up the process of enforcement by simply slowing down the publication of regulations in the Office of Management and Budget. Once the regulations were published, employers were bound to adhere to the standard.

So I agreed to very specific actions–agreements that technically I should not have been made to give. Sometimes huffing and puffing can win the battle, but lose the war. I was interested in the war.

The Senate took two months to confirm my nomination as Assistant Secretary in charge of three Divisions: Wage & Hour (WH), the Office of Federal Contract Compliance Programs (OFCCP), and Worker's Compensation (OWCP). The first Division was to ensure that employers followed proper guidelines in setting hourly wages, hours worked; the second was to ensure that federal contractors were adhering to affirmative action guidelines; and the third dealt with worker's compensation issues. I had my work cut out for me.

Years ago, I learned, House of Representative members George Crockett and Augustus "Gus" Hawkins had been involved in the effort to establish the Wage & Hour Division within Labor. Later, as I was confirmed, Gus Hawkins would say this to me: "We normally give the person in your job a lot of oversight. But we know where you stand. You don't have to worry about the Black Caucus bothering you."

I gathered courage from the people who went before me. I talked with every living predecessor–everyone who had been Assistant Secretary before me. Took each one out to dinner separately. The advice I got: Be independent. Get good people. And don't back away from any tough calls.

Some of the best advice I got was from Arthur Fletcher. He was my mentor, the first African American Assistant Secretary for Employment under the Nixon Administration. In fact, we had worked together when I was in the Nixon White House.

I knew Art. I knew that he had developed the Philadelphia Plan for Employment. It was the first plan of its kind in the country, and was the forerunner for all subsequent affirmative action plans. The Philadelphia Plan spelled out, in real numbers, the appropriate percentages of minorities to be hired as contractors and as employees on public sector-funded jobs. Art and his people had learned a lot trying to enforce that initiative.

It was amazing, the lengths to which companies and contractors went to skirt the requirement. They did something called "motorcycle compliance." If they knew that the auditors were coming to check, they'd run a group of minority workers to the site to be audited, then run them back to where they had been working. This way, they were able to use the same employees on different jobs. They didn't really have to be in compliance at all.

Art had to get more sophisticated. Looking back, it is amazing that they didn't do this in the beginning, but they instituted a procedure of checking actual employment records. Remember, this is affirmative action in its infancy. It didn't even occur to anyone that employers might try "motorcycle compliance" and other ways to get around justice. He was the first to do this kind of checking. I admired him.

And I appreciated his unique spin and perspective. He echoed the others, but his words carried even more weight. He was a pioneer. "Don't be afraid to make the tough decisions." I looked at him and knew: he had been there.

The legacy had been set. I had the confidence of my immediate superior, Elizabeth Dole, a long-standing Republican; and, on the other side, the Congressional Black Caucus. I had talked to every living person who had had the job before me. I was ready to go to work.

First, I followed my predecessors' advice and looked for, not just good people, but great people. I found them in the persons of:

Faye Anderson, a sister who'd grown up in the tough streets of Brooklyn. Stanford Law graduate. Had worked in Black Republican campaigns. Knew how to fight. Very, very smart. I hired her as my Special Assistant.

Bill Anderson (no relation), West Point, law degree from Vanderbilt, run and lost a race for the Senate. He was my point person on the reorganization–he was instrumental in making it happen.

Sam Walker, Phi Beta Kappa from Duke University, Harvard Law School. Had to lure him from a North Carolina law firm. When we had to have our late sessions, he would tell me, "I haven't stayed up all night since college." I picked him to be my attorney.

Cari Dominguez, former V.P. of Bank America. I hired her to run OFCCP.

I then took another kind of "birds-eye" view. How could we best get at the issues and come out of the gate fast? I thought back to the time I talked once to a veteran worker at GM, an assembly line worker. He came up with an idea that saved GM millions of dollars.

I asked him why he had not previously brought this idea to the attention of management. "No one ever asked me before," he replied. Finding out the employees' ideas was the key strategy to use. They knew best what was needed, what the problems were, how they could be solved.

I talked to both Andersons and to Sam Walker. We sent two surveys to more than 1,400 WH and OFCCP staff. They were designed to get to the heart of the matter. We asked for honest feedback, and we let the employees know that we valued their frank opinions about everything.

Those surveys got us up and running faster than I even could have imagined. We then held a Town Meeting for all staff to give everyone a chance to have their say and elaborate on their survey answers. I promised an Action Plan within thirty days of the Town Meeting–an ambitious goal, but achievable. I had learned through my industry experience that you can make things happen a lot faster than you think, when your survival depends on it. I appointed a Steering Committee to craft the plan from the surveys and Town Meeting. The plan they came up with was powerful, simple and easily understood. And it was measurable. Here it is, in plain English:

7-Point Action Plan

1- Top-down commitment to enforcement. Our area, Employment Standards, would send the message that the top leadership of the

Labor Department would have a razor-sharp focus on enforcing the laws that already existed. That would be the benchmark by which we would measure our actions and policies. Secretary Dole supported us every step of the way. She made the enforcement message clear from the outset in all her meetings with employees and in her public statements.

2-Quality, not just quantity. Sometimes you work just to get work out, but fail to ask whether you're working for the right things. I saw my role in terms of stewardship. I was given responsibility to steward, to take care of, take charge of, a process that I found to be flawed and ineffective. And stewardship demands quality–not just on doing things, but on doing the right things. We could say that we visited X number of businesses last year and made X number of citations, but were we really making a difference in the issues that mattered? Were workers really healthier and safer as a result of our work? Were children being adequately protected? And especially, were we focusing on the cases that would yield the maximum benefits for workers? Those are the kinds of questions we had to ask ourselves.

3-Appropriate distribution of resources. This goes to the quality question. We had to make sure that the things we wanted to make happen had the resources to make them happen. Again, busy-ness without effectiveness makes for a frustrated organization. And that is what we had in DOL in 1990.

4-Targeted prosecutions. This was critical. Who would we focus on prosecuting? We could expend our time and talent on small operators with little national impact, or we could go after the large employers. We could take a scattergun approach and have our investigators travel the country looking for violators, or we could focus on areas that history had proven were likely to contain employers known for past violations. We chose the latter, to great effect.

5-Enhanced Solicitor's services. Never before my tenure had the attorneys in the Solicitor's Office–the top law office within the Labor Department–been adequately informed about our monitoring activities and preliminary findings. For the first time, we put attorneys in all three divisions: Office of Federal Contract

Compliance, Wage & Hour, and Worker's Compensation. They sat in on all staff meetings. They were right there in the trenches, so they could hit the ground running whenever a prosecution presented itself. We kept them informed and involved, and they made themselves available to us.

6-Increased press coverage of enforcement. This was my personal favorite. There is nothing like the media to get people to change their behavior. We figured that, once companies knew that they would be caught and substantially fined for violations, they would start to clean up their acts. Our hunch proved right, and we did actually see substantial change in the areas that we targeted. Plus, it was a great educational tool. Not all corporate America is inherently evil; some actually did respond to the educational message we sent regarding what was allowable, especially in terms of child labor laws.

Our managers were happy as well. The administrators there never publicly received the credit they deserved for the hard work they did in finding violators and applying the remedies provided for by law. They finally got people to see their value, and it inspired them.

7-Emphasis on deterrence and voluntary compliance. We wanted to move companies to be proactive, to correct violations before we had a chance to discover them. I had worked in industry, and I knew the other side of the fence. It's just as true with people as with companies: permanent change is more likely if the change comes from within rather than from without.

With that blueprint for action, we could finally move. But there was one more major action to take. Our organization was a mess. We had Regional Administrators (RAs) who ran geographic areas who were responsible for operations and spending. Then, we had Program Heads in charge of policy, evaluation, and budget. Our staffpeople in the regional offices had to answer to both of these administrators. They had to run to the RAs to get approval to spend money, and to the Program Heads to address policy questions and concerns. Then, the RAs bumped up against the Program Heads when it came to finances, since RAs could spend but only Program Heads could budget. And as anyone knows, only monsters have two heads.

Then, there was the redundancy issue. I took a look at one particular communications document and counted how many people touched that letter. Eighteen initials were on that paper, representing eighteen hands through whom that paper passed on the way up the ranks. A response to that letter took the same number of people. It reminded me of the joke, "How many bureaucrats does it take to screw in a light bulb?"

The results were predictable. Confusing and contradictory communications. Staffers who didn't know which directive to follow. Arguments over turf. And a breakdown in our main priority: enforcement.

House Representative Augustus F. Hawkins, Chair of the Committee on Education and Labor and a member of the Black Caucus, saw the problem and was concerned. Further, he said that the RAs didn't seem to understand EEO (Equal Employment Opportunity) law or affirmative action. We met many times, and I was able to get his perspective and wisdom from long years of experience in government.

I keep going back to my corporate experience, but it was so valuable here. The action I took was swift and, to some, radical.

But first, there were small victories to be won. On the "eighteen-people-touching-one-piece-of-paper" problem, I simply asked those involved for their thoughts on how to change the process. The people who deal with a problem daily are closest to it, and will give the best answers. If we do not trust them enough to test ideas and even sometimes fail, something is wrong. No one can get ahead without making mistakes.

With small problems solved and incremental changes in place, I knew I had to prepare the way for the major organizational issues. Whenever you take radical action, you have to find a way to smooth the road that lies ahead. I went first to Secretary Dole, and then to key members of Congress to let them know my plans. I got my approvals upfront. I knew what kind of mess it would be if I failed to do that.

Then, in February of 1990 I called a meeting, inviting all 10 of my RAs to Airlie House, an idyllic retreat location in Virginia. Remember, I was preparing the way–not just to get the higher-ups to confirm my decision, but to get the staffers as well to sign-on, even as they knew they had no choice in the matter.

We started out with a nice lunch. I had only told one trusted RA what I would do. He was an RA in Dallas, and probably had the highest status within the group. He had won a top White House monetary award, and he really did lead the other RAs. He had their complete confidence. "I said to the RA based in Dallas: "Here's my plan. The system is not working, and we're going to have to change it. To do that I'm eliminating all the RA positions. We simply can't have our people reporting to two heads. I hope you understand." He assured me that he did, and that he would not whisper anything to a soul. I was grateful that he kept that promise.

I also offered him an opportunity to join my D.C. staff. He would have been a great addition. He opted to stay in Dallas.

The next day, I called them together. It was sort of like the Last Supper. Thirteen people: two Deputy Assistant Secretaries, myself, and 10 RAs. A sad announcement. Only one person knew other than myself. And I had been careful to write nothing on paper, nothing that anyone would be able to discover.

It was a hard but necessary housecleaning. Kind of like a surgical strike: short notice, strategic, quick, clean. The place I took them to had no televisions, no room phones (Fortunately for us, cell phones hadn't been invented yet).

I was well prepared. I even read the statement. That might seem unfeeling, but I didn't want to leave anything to chance, didn't want to say anything off the cuff that might have been misconstrued. I wanted to make sure we had our facts right. I wanted to make sure that the re-organization was tight. I didn't want any nit-picking on details we hadn't noticed. Bill Anderson and Sam Walker were invaluable here. They asked all the right questions and came up with a brilliant plan for reworking the entire division.

I was straightforward. Here is the statement, right to the point:

"THE REASON WE'RE HERE TODAY IS SO THAT I CAN LET ALL OF YOU KNOW THAT, AS OF RIGHT NOW, THE 10 REGIONAL ADMINISTRATOR JOBS HAVE BEEN ELIMINATED. I WILL SPEND THE REST OF THE DAY ONE-ON-ONE WITH EACH OF YOU, AND I WOULD LIKE FOR YOU TO THINK ABOUT WHERE YOU'D LIKE TO WORK. I WILL ATTEMPT TO ENSURE YOU THAT YOU WILL GET THE JOB YOU WANT."

The immediate reaction: *slack-jawed silence.* One attendee told me later, "We were dumbstruck." Understand, these administrators had the highest government-level positions possible in the system. Many had been in government service all their lives. They were well-connected. They knew senators. They knew presidents. They knew how to delay, how to slow the process, how to work the system. The Kansas City RA was one of Senator Dole's people. The RA who ran Boston had a close friend whose brother was a Massachusetts congressman. They really didn't think that I could pull this off. It really threw them off that I had done something they knew nothing about.

They asked me, "What are you going to do if this thing doesn't fly?" But I had done my homework. I had already checked with Elizabeth and her husband. I had already run it past the other key Senate and White House leaders. "This thing is already flying," I said to them.

The Massachusetts congressman was livid. I had testified at a Congressional hearing, and said that our operation was so efficient that we literally didn't need more money. He loved that. Gave me a beautiful pen. Then, I fired his best friend's brother, the Boston RA. "Bill," he said when he heard the news, "give me my damn pen back."

After lunch, there was dinner. That's where I was able to soften the blow. After all, this was not exactly a mass firing. It was more like a mass demotion. But to these powerful people, it must have felt like a firing.

At dinner, I explained to them that they had a choice. They could move to other positions within the Department, or they could take early retirements. I had brought along personnel people to meet with them individually and help them make their decisions.

I didn't count on the alcohol. A few industrious people brought liquor to our retreat. By the time I had gotten to the last group, they were liquored up–and fired up. For one woman, this job had given her a high profile in her urban community. When I asked her, "What do you think?" she replied, "What the hell do you think I think? You've taken away my credibility in the community!" She had once been a Catholic nun, and her ego was shattered.

Another RA accused me of discriminating against Hispanics. He was Hispanic, but the others weren't, so I chalked that up to anger, which was understandable.

I was sorry, but I couldn't worry about shattering egos. I was focused on the job we had to do. The people had to take care of themselves. But these were smart and savvy people. I knew they wouldn't be standing in bread lines. I had assured them that they could apply for other jobs within the system, but emphasized over and over that the Employment Standards organizational chart was simply unworkable as it stood. It really was.

But the staffers in the trenches were ecstatic. "This is the man who took out God!" they would tell me whenever I came to visit. This one action freed them to make decisions, gave them autonomy, and provided a clear line of authority for final approvals.

Then, I made another hard decision. She was an African American woman, the head of Wage & Hour. I remembered what Mrs. Parks had told me, about bringing other Blacks with me.

She didn't make it any easier. "You know I'm a Republican," she replied when I moved to replace her with another person. "Yes," I said, but you're a Reagan Republican, and this is a Bush Administration." I felt it was important to reinforce the message that this administration would be committed to employment justice and affirmative action. I was hell-bent on enforcing the law. I had to have someone who would vigorously seek to find and prosecute corporate lawbreakers, especially in the areas of child and farm labor. She was not the person for the job. So I had no choice. I had to fire her.

I did, however, keep her on temporarily as a consultant. She was angry, but I still was able to glean from her a perspective on the division and its current status. Admittedly, I needed that. I didn't know everything.

Gridlock was out. Action was in.

Breaking the "Glass Ceiling"

Having had the years of experience at GM, I knew what the workplace trends were. For an Assistant Labor Secretary, this was important. I knew about the demographics in terms of race, gender, and age. I knew that skilled workers were in short supply and high demand.

There had been a time when there were more than enough educated, motivated workers to choose from. America thought it could afford to leave some of its citizens undereducated, underskilled, and underutilized. All that was changing, and changing fast. Our challenge would be to assist in the effort to regain the nation's lost global competitiveness by recognizing and responding to the workforce changes.

At the same time, I saw an unprecedented opportunity to help those at the end of the line to take advantage of the opportunities that the country's skills gap offered. Ethnicity and color would have to take a back seat to training a productive workforce–and ethnic minorities and women had the most to gain here.

I managed to wrap my own personal goals and convictions around a larger agenda, and leverage the weight of the federal government to achieve both. In fact, at Labor, we were able to communicate a new message–that diversity is a business imperative, not just a social goal. We positioned ourselves as consultants, helping employers adapt to the workforce with training and skill building. Our message: every man or woman who wants a job can have one, if they have the skills.

Republicans are not known for their support of affirmative action. But this part of the Bush Cabinet, under Secretary Dole, worked to actually expand affirmative action initiatives. Our focus: quality. Our questions went from, "Are we making budget?" to Are we drawing the correct conclusions? Are we looking at the right things? Are we adding value to the country's labor table?"

We looked closely at industries that had few or no women and minorities and asked them, "Why?" Then, we helped them remove the obstacles to full participation in those companies.

First stop: the Glass Ceiling Initiative. The "Glass Ceiling" was the term used to represent this idea that women and minorities could only get so far in corporate America. They could see the positions to aspire to, but could never actually touch them. We wanted to address that problem.

It was like untangling a hard knot. Understand, there was no love lost between women's rights groups and the previous Reagan Administration. So when Secretary Dole delegated women's issues to me, the first thing I said to the initial groups was, "We're going to listen to you."

We had to listen. After all, by the time I came to Labor, more than half the jobs created since 1982 had been filled by women. Women were–and still are–the majority of workers in finance, insurance, real estate, banking, health and legal services. The number of women professionals had doubled since 1972, and the number of women in managerial jobs had almost tripled. Women-owned small businesses were growing at a rate five times those owned by men.

And listen we did. Over coffee. In formal and informal settings. In fact, one of the leaders said to me, "This is the first time we've been here in over eight years. We've never even had coffee; there was never enough time to sit down." What we found was that these women, no matter how well-educated, no matter what their age, no matter how thick their portfolios or credentials, felt they would never reach the top of their professions.

I loved talking to people. A community organization, "Back to Basics," made up of welfare mothers, called me. "We've watched you a long time. Nobody's ever come to our house–and we definitely can't get in the 'Big House'." I invited them to talk, and talk they did.

As we delved deeper into the initiative, I was surprised by the high level men who were supportive in corporate America. I found out why. They would tell me, "I've got a wife and a daughter in the workplace. I have to hear this discrimination stuff every night." They were weary of the tirades, and ready to listen because of the influence of the women in their lives.

Again, my work at GM helped. I had run succession planning, compensation, and bonus programs. I knew what to look for. We put together both affirmative action and glass ceiling reviews, and trained our investigators.

This was not an idle activity. We had a purpose in mind. The first thing we wanted to do was uncover facts. But the surveys we used did more than that. They actually helped companies self-assess their own positions and activities related to diversity. We turned the information we learned, not into a mechanism for punishment, but into an avenue for consulting and education.

But we used enforcement too. In the Reagan Administration, no companies were barred from doing business with the federal government because of their Equal Employment Opportunity violations. We turned that around, debarring a number of companies, often to their great surprise.

Lynn Martin, who replaced Elizabeth Dole as Secretary of Labor after Dole left for the Red Cross, issued a document, "A Report on the Glass Ceiling Initiative," in 1991. She didn't say it in her report, but we laid the groundwork for that initiative, actually called it into being. Its goals were lofty: we wanted to move corporations from adversaries to partners in the effort to ensure equal opportunity. We wanted to firmly link diversity to quality and performance in the workplace. We wanted to give the Department of Labor a clear set of blueprints to help them review corporations and assess their commitment to workplace diversity and equity.

The first thing we had to do was establish the need for such an initiative. We had our staff pore over three years of data from reviews we had conducted of Fortune 1000 companies. Establishing the facts was fairly straightforward. They told the story that we already knew: that minorities and women had a tenuous foothold in the managerial and executive suites. Specifically, we found that women held only 16.9% of managerial positions, and minorities only 6%. We found that, at the executive levels, the respective figures were 6.6% and 2.6%. We cited a 1990 survey conducted by the University of California at Los Angeles Anderson Graduate School of Management and Korn/Ferry International, an executive search firm, that revealed only slight increases of minorities and women in top executive positions within the Fortune 1000 companies: from less than 3% to less than 5%. Minority women made up 3.3% of women corporate officers and only 1-2% of all corporate officers.

And these were only general averages. Certain sectors, such as manufacturing, weighed in with even lower percentages than these.

We knew we had a tough battle, so we started at the same place where, years ago, a small cadre of military officers began an effort to address racial issues: with education. We met with business, trade and professional organizations, some that represented minorities and women. We met with human resources staff and business leaders all over the country. It helped us to understand the issues better from all perspectives.

We learned a lot in this first step of the process. We learned that there would have to be a top-down commitment to the effort at the corporate level. We learned that confidentiality would be extremely important as we began collecting data. We learned that the Department of Labor (DOL) officials who conducted the reviews would have to spend enough time at a company to learn its culture before drawing any conclusions. We came to understand that it would be critical to meet with the highest officials in the corporation and not stop at the level of EEO (Equal Employment Opportunity) officer.

We then moved to select nine corporations for pilot management reviews. We chose them, not according to their diversity "numbers," but in order to get a broad cross-section of companies both geographically and in terms of products and services. In these reviews, we would be able to determine whether there were artificial barriers that prevented upward mobility according to ethnicity or gender. We would be able look at which companies voluntarily worked to remove those obstacles if they existed. And we would learn the best way to conduct the reviews once we rolled out the process.

My previous background with the Labor Department, and at General Motors, was a great help here. One of my positions at GM was as Director of Personnel Planning on the corporate labor relations staff. I had also served as General Director, Personnel and Public Relations at the Delco Moraine Division in Dayton, Ohio. I understood what a good succession plan looked like. I knew how to evaluate compensation systems, and how to develop a process that would uncover possible inequities.

So we laid the groundwork for the study. Lynn Martin and her staff implemented and reported the results. The report was very specific–DOL staff were looking, not for broad statistical numbers of the entire employee population, but for equity in the selection of a select and elite group: those who would run the organization. The staff took care to look closely, for example, at how the managerial ranks highly populated by minorities and women moved past middle management into upper management. Was there a formal process? Was the succession planning more or less reliant on the "old boys network?" These are the kinds of questions the staff had to answer. And playing a simple numbers game would not uncover that kind of information.

We made clear to the companies we reviewed that we were not looking to change their culture or basic business practices, but instead to help them consider and implement approaches that would improve advancement opportunities for minorities and women.

The Department found some typical and troubling patterns. In one company, a woman who had an MBA was put into a non-managerial career path. DOL staff asked why this was, and the reply was typical: "Well, she moved here for personal reasons, so we assumed ..." It was an assumption made all too often.

The DOL staff involved in the reviews discovered that the so-called "glass ceiling" was even lower than they had anticipated. They started their work looking at the top jobs; when they found no women or persons of color even close to those positions, they shifted their focus to analyzing the pipeline that led to those jobs. They also found that women tended to be placed higher than minorities. The only exception was in the high-tech or scientific fields, where color and gender took second place to technical skill and training. These skills were so rare and so needed that discrimination was obviously and glaringly counterproductive.

The next level of discovery provided much revelation on the infrastructure that worked to preclude diversity. DOL staff found that, while companies considered it a business necessity to identify and develop key employees that would become tomorrow's corporate leaders, there was no such "business necessity" attached to equal employment opportunity and access. The reviewers found scant records related to individual employee training and development histories; there was no way to uncover the standard "tracts" that companies followed to groom these key employees. No formal systems existed to monitor individuals' credential-building experiences. No one seemed to know how top-level managers actually "got there."

Sometimes beginning the remedy was as simple as assigning one person to ensure that a representative number of minorities and women were invited to participate in high-exposure training programs, job rotations, committee assignment, and the like. In other companies, the evaluation/compensation systems were incredibly loose. The report completed by DOL under Martin noted:

"One company used a narrative performance appraisal system for employees at certain levels with no guidelines or standards to follow. This subjective appraisal system left much to the rating official's discretion. While evaluations of men were directed toward performance, female appraisals at times were stereotypical. One woman remarked she never knew how she was doing because her appraisals had such things as happy,'friendly,' and 'gets along well with others."

-A Report on the Glass Ceiling Initiative, 1991, U.S. Department of Labor, p. 15

When the reviewer pointed this out, the company in question changed to a more objective rating process.

No company in the pilot study had ever reviewed their compensation packages to uncover evidence of discrimination or ensure non-discrimination. This would be an important component in the Department's continuing education with companies; it was already well-documented that whites tended to rate minorities and women less favorably, independent of job performance.

Then there was the issue of tracking. Jobs in human resources and public relations rarely led to the top office. That corporate-styled "ghetto" is where many minorities and women found themselves. Sometimes a quick look at ethnic and gender comparisons relative to job type were enough to gauge a company's commitment to diversity. Companies that had few minorities and women in "line" positions (sales and marketing, production) as opposed to staff positions (sales support functions, human resources) were asked to conduct placement audits to ensure fair representation in all job categories.

The reviewers also found that companies had often woefully inadequate records to even make a fair determination relative to Equal Employment Opportunity/Affirmative Action guidelines. The staff stressed to companies that their status as government contractors required rigorous record keeping.

The pilot study identified a number of barriers to the advancement of minorities and women-barriers that even Fortune 500 CEOs concede exist. Here were just a few:

- Informal and subjective selection procedures.
- "Home grown" senior level executives (individuals who had been with the company for more than 25 years, when practically no minorities or women were in management-track positions)
- Over-reliance on word-of-mouth references to fill top positions and hiring outside the formal recruitment process. (The "Old Boy Network")
- Failing to inform their executive search firms of their affirmative action obligations/commitment.

- Failing to make employees aware of the highest-level executive positions.
- Holding interviews in hotel rooms–a practice that discourages many women, who find the prospect of interviewing with a man in a hotel room intimidating.
- Allowing individual managers to follow their own processes for grooming their successor.
- No formal mentoring effort with guidelines and benchmarks–every "mentor" is allowed to follow their own course with their proteges, and is given complete freedom even in choosing whom they wish to mentor.
- Failure to make diversity everyone's responsibility, not just the EEO/Affirmative Action Officer's.

The companies that responded most enthusiastically were those who were open to employment diversity but did not know how to implement such an effort. These companies agreed to begin such practices as aggressive recruitment strategies; using "deputy" assignments to groom minorities and women for high-level positions; embarking on formal mentoring programs that targeted high–performing minorities and women; and introducing accountability-that is, incorporating progress on diversity into executives' review and compensation packages.

I am proud of the fact that our group within Labor helped to crystallize and clarify this issue. Now, corporate executives around the globe are calling diversity a "business imperative."

Taking on Child Labor Violators

When I think about our experiences going after child labor violators, I think about 13-year-old Matthew Garvey of North Dakota. He was working in a car wash–something he was definitely too young to do–and had his leg accidentally sheared off when he mishandled some of the controls. The car wash was fined $733.00 for its initial violation, then another whopping $1,800.00 when the Office of Safety and Health Administration (OSHA) went back and found that Matthew was still working there. A grand total of $2,533.00 for a boy's leg.

After doing some digging, I found out that the average fine for child fatalities in the workplace was $740.00 Labor had found 59 such child fatalities (children under the age of 19) in 1987 and 1988. Who knows how many others went unreported and undiscovered?

I dug further and found other problems. I had a teacher tell me that young teens were sleeping in class because they had worked the day or night before.

Contrast this with the situation in Japan, where 1% of all schoolchildren work at jobs. Their real work is schoolwork–they spend an average of 25 hours per week doing homework. Here in the United States, 34% of our schoolchildren work; and they spend 4 hours per week doing homework. A typical progression, and this is for a good student, is this: Sophomore year: all A's. Junior year: a job, all B's. Senior year: a car, all C's. Those are the priorities, and the grades reflect them. And we wonder why international differences in math scores and academic achievement are most pronounced at the high school level?

A Washington Post reporter approached me one day, to explain another phenomenon. "Bill, are you up on this candy stuff? Let me tell you what really happens." It was about children who approach adults in the street or door-to-door, saying that they're fund raising for their college education or some other worthy cause. Turns out they're actually making money for some unscrupulous entrepreneur waiting in a van for the children to bring their money back. If they are relying on that money for college, they can forget it.

These experiences ignited my passion to find child labor violators. Our laws are pretty liberal for teen workers. Children under 16 can work three hours a day on school days. On non-school days, they can work eight hours. During the summer, they can work an adult-sized 40 hours per week. And they can only work between 7am and 7pm.

In terms of farm work, no child under 12 was allowed to work in the fields; and no child under 14 was allowed to work for farmers who grow for the major food companies like Campbell or Heinz.

But our companies weren't able to meet even these generous standards. In 1989, Labor found twice as many illegally employed minors as it did in 1982. The reason? Demographics. Fewer available workers between the ages of 16 and 24 (a decline of about 2 million over a ten-year period) led to increased hiring violations by employers seeking workers at any cost.

When done right, a task force can be a wonderful thing. But it is important to leave with some concrete tasks and actions. We formed a Task Force at Labor, to better collect information on child labor practices, and to improve coordination and enforcement. We then reviewed restrictions on hazardous occupations in order to update the regulations for the most dangerous jobs.

We ended up increasing fines and penalties by 60-300% for violators, and even heavier financial penalties for the most egregious offenders. To further address the problem, we increased our use of preliminary and permanent injunctions for serious violators or offenders who demonstrated an unwillingness to comply with the law.

Meanwhile, back at the House of Representatives, Rep. Tom Lantos (D) was gearing up for a fight. His House Subcommittee on Child Labor was releasing vitriolic statements of criticism for Labor's apparent (to him) inattention and lack of data.

His criticism proved unnecessary. Less than 24 hours earlier, we announced a three-day child labor "strike force." Five-hundred inspectors would visit 3,900 companies in 49 states plus Washington, DC and Puerto Rico. Half our enforcement staff was out looking for child labor violators during that period.

We made substantial headway. We uncovered 7,000 illegally employed minors among 1,400 companies in three days. We found Burger King a major violator of the "hours worked" regulations. Apparently a lot of the kids sleeping in class had been working at Burger King the night before. We fined them $500,000, the largest child labor settlement at that time levied against a single company. We were able to impact their 800 company-owned stores by directing them, in addition to paying the fine, to create a model employment practice for double-checking minor children's ages. We appointed an independent official to oversee compliance, set up a computer system to track hours worked, and opened an 800 line for workers to call with complaints or concerns. Interestingly, most of the violators we caught were in the suburbs, not the city.

Altogether, we assessed $3.6 million in civil penalties to companies who were typically working 14-15 year-olds too hard and employing 16-17 year-olds in hazardous jobs. We busted more violators in three days than in the previous two years.

The second strike focused on the "City of Angels," Los Angeles. The word got out that we were there to find and prosecute violators. I had the temerity to walk into the lion's den: a fast food association meeting. Many looked quizzically at me; one even asked if I were in the right room. Their question for me: "Why are you keeping these young people from supporting their families?"

What a question, I thought. How had they managed to turn an illegality, a affront to our youth, into a compassionate act? But I had done my homework, and I had an answer.

"Only twenty percent are doing that," was my reply. "The rest are out buying cars, sneakers, and stereos."

Children working on farms was a more difficult problem. We found that most violations involving farm workers' children went unreported. With more than 250,000 such children in the country, this was a major concern.

But it was harder to enforce. Who can a poor migrant worker leave their children with? They can't afford child care. They often lack transportation to carry their children to school. Many of their relatives are working right along with them. So they bring their children along, just to make sure they're safe.

"Everyday our children spend working in the fields is another day in which they lose their precious childhood, another day exposed to pesticides and workplace dangers, another day lost to education. It is not only a national loss, it is a national shame." Farm Labor Organizing Committee President Baldemar Velasquez said that during the time we were investigating this issue, and I couldn't agree more. When we talk about child labor issues, we're really talking about the future of America.

To complicate matters, there was not just one standard. Every state was unique in terms of types of violators, strength of state enforcement activity, and stringency of laws and regulations. Some of the states had even stricter regulations than Labor. New York was just one example. They had strict child labor laws, an aggressive enforcement mechanism, and the spotlight of the media on sweatshops, especially in the garment district.

Yet, despite all the attention and focus, we were not able to find the child labor violators in the garment district. We knew they were there. Perhaps *they* knew *we* were there. We worked closely with the state of New York's Labor Department. Secretary Dole would visit the garment district anonymously and unannounced. I spoke fluent French, and there were a lot of French-speaking blacks in the garment district. When I greeted them with "Bonjour," the managers went crazy. We left nothing to chance.

It is my great regret that we did not make more headway in New York. We knew they were hiring kids, but we couldn't find the kids. In other states, such as Missouri, Illinois, and Pennsylvania, we had major drops in violation rates after the first "strike force" had ended; in others, there seemed to be almost no impact.

Don't get me wrong. There were embarrassments. News reporter Andrea Mitchell came to my office once to talk about child labor. She brought the news cameras with her. When I found out what she was up to, I wished she hadn't.

"Don't you have small children down in Tampa picking oranges?" she asked. I was confident. We had done so much work in this area, I thought I knew. "I've got my people all over there," I replied. Then, the statement that plastered me all over the evening news: "There are no children picking oranges there."

Fast forward to that night: a split screen. On one side: making my statement. On the other side? Children picking oranges in Tampa. She had set me up. She already knew the truth, and wanted a way to embarrass the department. I had helped her. I bit–hard.

I was so angry, I wrote a letter to the President of NBC. All the PR people in the office begged me not to. But I really believed that this had been done for drama, for effect. Sometimes, you just have to tell people what you really think of them. I'm not sure it helped. It may even have hurt. But it sure felt better.

A short-lived "better," however. I remember going into Tom Lantos's Subcommittee. Andrea Mitchell was there, with a friendly "Good morning, Mr. Secretary." In fact, after that letter, any time I appeared before a Subcommittee, she made it her business to be there.

They brought in a young person who'd been hurt in a work-related accident. Then parents of a child who died in an unsafe work environment.

Lantos pointed his finger at me. "Don't you have any humanity?" That, too, was on the evening news.

I learned I couldn't win. You almost never can with the press. But I never regretted writing that letter. And, for the most part, I was able to maintain good relations with the press–mostly by providing the information and quotes they needed when they needed them.

But Lantos and I eventually became more cooperative colleagues. We continued one of our Congressional Hearing conversations on radio. Later, he called me and told me I was "pretty good."

I did, later, have a much better experience. This time, I was on the other side of the fence. The show was ABC's "Good Morning America." My opposing guest, Jack Fischer, Owner/Manager of a Shakey's Pizza, was publicly wondering why we at Labor had to go after teenagers for merely trying to work and make extra money. I retorted that we were ensuring the health, well-being, and educational advancement of the young workers we were trying to protect. It was true: teachers were reporting that kids were coming to school and falling asleep because they had worked late into the night at Burger King or McDonald's. The money they made couldn't possibly be worth it–to them or to our nation.

He put his foot in his mouth when he suggested that he knew he was breaking the law. He seemed to think people would wink at his bending of the rules. When one of his young employees, Becky Gregg, came on the show saying, "No one should tell us how many hours we should work"–and she was under 17!–I felt that the public would back what we were trying to do.

Down on the Farm

In the Senate confirmation hearings, my nemesis and eventual friend, Senator Howard Metzenbaum, asked me, "What do you know about farm labor?" "Remember, I'm from Michigan," I replied. "I don't know anything about it."

His staffer schooled me. "Take a trip over to mid-Michigan and look at the apple orchards. Fly over to Toledo and check out the cucumber farms. Then tell me what you find out."

That staffer was smart. I found that some of the smartest congressional staffers worked for Metzenbaum and Ted Kennedy. This guy eventually ended up at General Electric, where he serendipitously met up with my daughter, who was working there. "Are you related to Bill Brooks?" he asked. "Yes, that's my father," she said. "I helped get your father confirmed at Labor," he boasted. I couldn't believe that the staffer of the senator who gave me so much trouble would actually form his lips to say that, but he did.

We learned a lot just "walking around" the farm labor areas across the country. Secretary Dole went to cucumber farms in Zellwood, Florida and a nearby migrant camp. We then started a whirlwind tour from June to October. We toured peach farms in South Carolina, berry farms in New Jersey, tobacco and cucumber farms in North Carolina, tomato and pepper farms in Virginia, Maryland, and Delaware, potato and fruit farms in Pennsylvania. We were appalled by what we found.

We undertook 1,200 investigations covering 11,200 farmworkers. We went after cases that we had the highest probability of winning. Farm Labor Contractors (FLCs) who had previously been cited for violations. FLCs never before investigated. Areas that had historically high violation rates. Areas whose registrations had been revoked. Housing camps. The result: we found in favor of

1,028 workers who were owed $75,000 in back wages–one of the highest conviction rates on record at Labor. And we collected almost a half million dollars in civil penalties. We came up with a very effective on-the-spot assessment, kind of like a police ticket, that worked well for mobile employers who had been assessed relatively small fines. We were able to collect many of those right on the spot. Then, we developed a new strategy that allowed us to bond FLCs to ensure that they would make back wage payments–kind of an insurance policy against them shortchanging workers.

Then we took on what I like to call "Big Sugar." The state of Florida has the nation's largest population of temporary, foreign agricultural workers. At the time we were involved, that number exceeded 10,000. I remember one sugar farm we visited. It was in Palm Beach City, where 80% of Florida's sugar cane is produced. Black Americans did that harvesting work before World War II, but the immigrants from South America had taken their place. These were the worst working conditions I had ever seen in my life. Cuban families controlled these farms, and they ruled with an iron hand. I remember Secretary Dole telling me, "You're going to end up under one of these sugar cane plants." I was afraid that I might. When one of the farm managers asked me if I was staying for the night, I quickly mentioned that I would be heading out.

We then developed a 152-page plan to improve farm worker conditions. It was comprehensive and, to some, radical. Secretary Dole sent the plan to Roger Porter, President Bush's Chief Domestic Affairs Adviser; and Edith Holiday, Secretary of the Cabinet. The plan called for near-daily enforcement strikes, and emphasized the serious problem of pesticide poisoning.

The White House didn't like it. They were getting pressure from the big agricultural employers, and they were listening.

Later, *Newsweek* magazine called to find out what had happened to the farm labor plan. I had to say honestly that I didn't know. I didn't have real evidence, but I really did know: it died in the system, killed by the farm lobby.

There were other actions. Randolph Thomas Nicholas, an African American carpenter, was one of the most memorable. Nicholas claimed that the Washington Metro Area Transit Authority in Washington, D.C. had discriminated against him. They claimed that his high blood pressure was the reason he was not hired. (High blood pressure? How many more blacks would be out of a job if that were the criteria?)

We made the Transit Authority hire him in 1990, with back pay extending to 1978, when he had been turned down for the job. It amounted to more than $300,000. Plus, we made them give him the pay and seniority he would have had he been initially hired in 1978.

We wanted to make it cheaper *not* to discriminate.

Then there was the University of Maryland at College Park. This was a hard one. The university had a solid record for diversity in hiring faculty and recruiting/enrolling students. You couldn't paint them as "racist" with a broad brush. However, they clearly were not making any headway when it came to hiring African Americans and Asians for secretarial and clerical positions. And so we imposed penalties and insisted that they put appropriate remedies in place to fix the problem.

There was a reason we went after the university. Universities, especially major institutions, are large employers. If we turn them around, we impact a lot of people. And they set an example for the students, many of whom will eventually make hiring and firing decisions. Again, targeting for impact–looking at how we can affect as many as possible through our enforcement practices.

Picking On an Icon

Why pick on the Salvation Army? After all, their job was to minister to those with the greatest needs. Shouldn't they be free to do their job without interference from 'stickler' bureaucrats?

I heard all those arguments when we decided to take on the Salvation Army. And then I learned what an army they actually were.

In 1990, a gentleman by the name of Admiral Cooney served as chair of the charitable organization Goodwill, and had also been appointed to chair the Committee on Sub-Minimum Wage Rules. He wrote the Labor Department, complaining that the Salvation Army did not follow the federal minimum wage guidelines. A disgruntled Salvation Army worker managed to secure and send to us some confidential documents that were very incriminating and would help further make that case.

Apparently, the Salvation Army was putting to work many of the drug-addicted and homeless people they took into their shelters. Helping around the shelter with cleaning and other maintenance activities was considered part of their responsibility in return for a roof over their heads and food. But they also provided a nominal amount of "pin money"–sometimes as little as $20 a week.

That "pin money" was the problem. Sometimes companies hired handicapped workers to do selected simple tasks; for that, they were allowed to pay less than minimum wage. Federal guidelines said that only in this kind of "sheltered workshop" situation could the minimum wage requirement be set aside.

But we did not necessarily consider the Salvation Army workers to be handicapped. Since they were, in effect, being paid for work, no matter how menial, we felt that we were obligated to investigate, and enforce the law if necessary.

I wrote the national head of the Salvation Army. We arranged a meeting on their turf in New York City, an "L.A. Law"-type office, richly appointed. We knew then that the humble Salvation Army had some power behind it.

The Army top brass began very courtly. We started with prayer. I stated our case, explained the problem, then asked them what they intended to do.

The mood changed very quickly. The Salvation Army chair retorted, "I guess we have to get rid of the President to get rid of you." And then, "Someone bigger than us is going to take care of us." They scared our staffers. Who, they thought, could this "bigger" entity be? What kind of threat were they?

The Chair proved to be right in his prediction. When they got wind of the Labor Department's suit against the Salvation Army, papers no less than the *Wall Street Journal* and the *Washington Post* took up their case. One *Post* writer even told me later, "I tried to do a positive story on Labor's perspective, but 'they' wouldn't let me." I never was quite sure who 'they' were; whoever they were, they wielded power from a mysterious but effective place.

I really was trying to enforce the law and make sure that everyone adhered–even well-intentioned organizations like the Salvation Army. The Army's argument was that, since most of their workers were either on drugs or had mental disorders, they qualified as "sheltered market" workers as these were considered disabilities. I felt this was a stretch, but I did try to work with them. Goodwill Industries had the same issue, but they had gone through the right channels and received a waiver based on the special contingencies of their arrangements with workers. I urged the Salvation Army to do the same thing, and offered to provide the same remedy. But they wouldn't budge. So I wouldn't either.

Congresswoman Marge Roukema from New Jersey was especially hot. She called me a "rascal," only half joking. I told her that if Congress changed the law, I would be able to lay off the Salvation Army. Then I got called to the White House. John Sununu, White House Chief of Staff at the time, called for me to explain.

We ended up in the Virginia Courthouse. Ultimately, we backed away from fully enforcing the law there. I was not sorry that we moved to enforce the law in every nook and cranny; but I was actually kind of relieved that we did not have to fully take them on. After all, who would have thought that the men and women who ring bells at the malls represented such a powerful organization?

Looking back over my 18-month stint as Assistant Secretary of Labor, I can still smile. No blood was shed in the reorganization, and we still managed to save about $4 million a year in staff and related costs. I was proud of my ESA staff for accommodating and catalyzing change. In effect, I think we managed to reenergize the department to work toward the next set of goals. In all things, our job was to make sure that American workers–all American workers–kept the faith. We wanted them to know that we were on the job. I am spurred by a long-held promise to give back to the communities of America, and by my conviction that the American workforce, properly trained and properly motivated, has no equal in the world.

People always say “you can’t make anything happen in government.” I disagree. You have to be decisive. You have to surround yourself with smart and committed people. But you can make it happen.

Chapter Four

GM: A New Way of Seeing

When I left Labor, I moved into a top-management position at General Motors. I did not, however, leave behind my passion for racial equality. On the heels of an innovative and successful effort to create an institution within the military to address race relations and racism, and a major effort to address multiple discriminatory challenges at Labor, I wanted to see how I would be able to mount a similar effort at GM.

GM hired me as Executive Director of Personnel and Administration for Global Truck Operations and moved my family back to Detroit. I knew that my prior employment history would go before me and engender a certain amount of respect and confidence in my abilities. But I wanted more than that. I wanted to make a difference by introducing new ideas. I wanted to change the system. I wanted to beat the system.

What better way to do that than to develop a new perspective on an old issue? I had worked, in the 1970's, with noted sociologist and author Jay Nisberg to begin seeding the idea that discrimination adversely affects employee behavior, and suggest that companies that discriminate are simply damaging themselves. But I did it in terms that were understood and appreciated by the world in which I operated. Most people in the field of human resources and behavioral science were familiar with Abraham Maslow's theory of the hierarchy of needs: that human beings needed first to survive, then to be safe, then to be socially involved, then to have a positive self-concept, then to be self-actualized.

Maslow applied this hierarchy to all persons, regardless of ethnicity or gender. I decided to advance another theory, a theory that would apply to African Americans in particular, based on the observations I had made as an African American person.

But before putting forth the theory in the article itself, I was able to get in this "zinger": "If management action in industry is arbitrary and arouses uncertainty of continued employment or reflects favoritism or discrimination, the employee's behavior will be influenced because of his need for safety in the employment relationship."

In our current era of corporate downsizing and job-hopping, this statement would not have been so dramatic. But in the '70s, when people were still depending on one employer for life and just as racism and discrimination were starting to be acknowledged and addressed in corporate America, this was a powerful argument against discrimination–an argument that began to look at the "boomerang" effect of discrimination in the marketplace.

Yet I did want to reveal a side of African American life that many African Americans hesitated to talk about or acknowledge. I made the case that we as African Americans tended toward a "pattern of conspicuous behavior and conspicuous consumption," a behavior designed to maintain a "front" as an acceptable substitute for actually "getting ahead" in the economic sense. "Black leaders everywhere since the Civil War," Nisberg and I argued in a respected sociology magazine, "are constantly urging the community to raise its sights above survival, having a good time and praising God. They present getting ahead as a racial duty as well as a personal gain.

And that went to our next point: to put forth a slightly different take on Maslow's "higher needs" theory. We called it the "Brooks/Nisberg Need Hierarchy" and contrasted it to Maslow's.

We made it clear that this was not a new concept–especially the concept that "Upgrading the Race" was at the pinnacle of the African American needs hierarchy. In fact, Samual M. Strong wrote an unpublished Ph.D. thesis on the topic in 1940 when he was at the University of Chicago, entitled "The Social Type Method: Social Types in the Negro Community of Chicago."

We talked about the daily struggle of many African Americans to survive, in light of efforts to lock them out of the "good jobs." We talked about the struggle as largely unconscious, brought to the forefront of consciousness generally by the internal force of depression or the more external/social phenomenon of race rioting.

We then moved to the concept of "having a good time" or enjoying life as a release from the daily grind of survival. It was an outlet, a real need in the black community. We felt it was time to recognize, describe and explain this characteristic to the larger community. "Absorption in pleasure," we explained, "is a kind of adjustment to [African Americans'] subordinate status in American life."

We then brought the importance of the black church to bear on our new hierarchy of needs. We explained statistically that African Americans have more churches and ministers per capita than their white counterparts.

"Getting ahead" ranked higher in the hierarchy. This simply meant that African Americans tended to see the church as a basic need, a backbone in a racist and challenging world. Once this need was met, blacks could move on to their own personal and professional fulfillment. It was then, and only then, that African Americans could look to a wider community and take on the more altruistic mantle of "Upgrading the Race." Remember, the Civil Rights Movement only took off after blacks had managed to migrate North and take advantage of the relatively higher-paying factory opportunities that the North represented. When blacks began to do better as a whole, the struggle for black equality unleashed itself. We made the observation that "Most white people are only occasionally aware of blacks" while most blacks "live in a state of intense and perpetual awareness that they are a black minority in a white man's world."

We went even further: "'Race consciousness' is not the work of 'agitators' or 'subversive influences.' It is forced upon blacks by the very fact of their separate-subordinate status in American life." We talked about the constant externally-applied pressure that African Americans labored under to "prove" themselves not inferior, to themselves as well as to the larger (white) community. As a result, we said "Beating the white man at his own game becomes a powerful motivation for achievement." We comb the statistics for evidence that the employment, education, and living standards/income gaps between blacks and whites are closing. Once we are satisfied with basic needs, we typically move on to improving the fate of those who look like us. That explained, we concluded, the African American fascination with black "heroes"–in essence a vicarious way to self-vindication.

Some would argue that this is no longer the case, that the "highest" need level of "saving the race" has become passe. To some extent, I would have to agree. Many African Americans in the new generations are not as interested in giving back. I salute those to whom this trend does not apply. I think about Darien Dash, the young African American entrepreneur with a publicly-held company that is aggressively addressing the problem of the "Digital Divide," the troubling gap between technology use by African Americans vs. whites. We do have our young heroes. But they are rare, and we need more.

By the 1990s, the automobile industry had seen a lot. It had seen its market share eroded over a twenty-year period to more nimble, customer- and quality-minded Japanese automobile companies. It had experienced something of a comeback in the '80s, but was operating in a recessionary period–not as devastating as the '70s, but still unsettling and still a phenomenon that had to be addressed.

It was that atmosphere to which I returned after I left Labor. And I knew we needed a new way to look at things, a new way of seeing.

In the Spring of 1991, I spoke at SER Metro-Detroit, a Hispanic social service organization involved in literacy, child care, and employment skills training. I cited a number of inevitable, unavoidable new developments with critical implications for business:

- First, fewer new workers would be available to industry; Second, those reduced workers would be older;
- Third, there would be more women, minorities, and immigrants in this new labor pool;
- Fourth, the jobs available would be more service and information-oriented than manufacturing-oriented;
- Fifth, those jobs would require much higher educational and skill levels than ever.

At the time, this was news. The business community was just beginning to take note and craft a strategic response. It was my personal mission to make sure GM responded in a way that would keep the company competitive.

The conclusion I drew from these developments was what I shared with the SER-Metro audience of industry and social service supporters: "...business simply cannot afford to waste talent or America will become a third-rate has-been." The talents, skills, and abilities of minorities and women had been, at best, ignored and at worst, undermined by a society that continued many of its racist and sexist practices, even in light of the disastrous effects on the entire nation. That was going to have to change.

I felt we had made some inroads in Washington during the short two years of my tenure as Assistant Secretary of Labor. I was excited about the prospect of bringing the lessons learned there back to my long-term employer. I felt there some critical things needed attention. At the forefront of my mind was the issue that we had begun to dig into at Labor: the issue of diversity.

Those who believed in diversity and social change could no longer get away with a simply altruistic argument. We had to merge the social agenda with the agenda of the corporate community in order to make diversity a working reality. I felt we began that process, and my goal was to make the connection unavoidably and unarguably clear to top management.

I pointed out first to management that the concept of diversity was not a new one. In 1911, GM established an export company to supply products to wholesale distributors around Europe and the globe. In 1923, they opened its first assembly plant in Copenhagen. They acquired European automotive companies Vauxhall Motors and Adam Opel in the 1930s. By 1960, seven of eight vehicles sold by GM overseas were managed abroad. For the 1990s, I wanted to position GM as a "world leader" in transportation products and services.

I made the case that the concept of "world leader" as we approached the 21st century would have to be framed in a different light. The face of leadership was slowly becoming more colorful and more diverse. A "world leader" could not be led solely by white males of European ancestry. First, any company that called itself a world leader with such a monolithic employment base would immediately become suspect. Secondly, such a group could not effectively lead representing a group that made up less than 20% of the world's population. After all, we had already seen statistics that indicated white males would be only 15% of the incoming new employees. A company that did not recognize the value of diversity in its employment as well as its leadership would be severely hamstrung competitively.

Plus, we knew that growing diversity in our customer base would naturally lead to a diverse work force, and drive an increasing global perspective. This was a "business imperative," I told them-the same word I had used so often at the Labor Department.

GM's top brass bought the argument. It was time to get to work.

The challenge that confronted us was how to create and maintain an environment that naturally allowed for the full contribution of the entire GM community–employees, dealers, suppliers–as we pursued total customer satisfaction. It would require a massive effort; after all, we were trying to change the culture of an organization. We would have to benchmark, learn from other companies and from experts in the field. We would have to mount a company-wide global communication and training effort.

I worked closely with noted diversity "guru" Roosevelt Thomas, an author and consultant highly respected in the field by both the private and public sector, to craft a strategy. Our mission was to be seen as world leaders in our area. Our vision was total customer *enthusiasm*. Notice I did not say "satisfaction". Satisfied customers leave with a smile. They may write a nice note to a person's manager. Enthusiastic customers talk you up to other people who may not be customers. They respect the statements that come out of company headquarters. They consider you as they look for employment. The better they are in their field, the more likely they are to consider a "world class" employer.

As we began to communicate our mission and vision throughout the organization, we knew also that we would have to instill certain core values in our employees. We wanted to attract and keep creative people who had a pioneering spirit. We wanted them to use that spirit to innovate and think "outside the box," and we knew that this would only happen as employees challenged the rules instead of blindly following them. We wanted to see breakthrough thinking and a mentality that moved us to improve continuously. The Japanese are experts at this, with their emphasis on an industry term that means continuous improvement, "Kaizen." We Americans go for the home run, and strike out a lot; the Japanese tend to go for bunts, singles and steals. It's those incremental improvements over time that are the most powerful.

Then, we wanted our employees to feel comfortable with change, and with diversity. And remember, we would be working with a population base that was getting older, not younger. The values we sought to instill were much more familiar to persons in younger age brackets, and so our goal presented an additional challenge.

One of our first actions under this new model and vision was to conduct a cultural assessment. In order to introduce change, you have to know where your employees are. From that assessment, we developed our strategy. In marketing, we would give our divisions a mandate to develop products that reflected the needs and desires of a diverse market. Marketing research, reports, focus groups–all would have to demonstrate that they were paying attention to all demographic groups.

This brought about a natural development in our base of suppliers and marketing contractors. At the end of the day, we found ourselves hiring African American and Hispanic companies. They developed a program that carried out this part of the mission.

I am proudest of the fact that we did indeed end up with major increases in the diversity of our supplier base. It echoed a strategy originally crafted by the founder of one of GM's biggest competitors: Ford Motor Company. Henry Ford took the then-revolutionary step of paying workers $5 a day to move up north. 'If they are making money,' he reasoned, 'they'll buy cars.'

We all know how well that strategy worked. This was simply an extension of that strategy to another arena. Instead of creating employees that would buy our products, we were creating entire industries where none had been before. These new and growing companies would of course hire more employees. Many of those employees, who worked for companies for whom GM was their bread and butter, would make it their business to purchase GM products.

As we were knee-deep in the process of making change–of "beating the system"–I also wanted to make sure the world knew that we were changing. If the world knew, if various communities that had impact and clout knew, GM would have to be accountable. Once you have rolled out change, it is important to make it public.

I spoke to any group that would have me: universities, industry associations, community groups. I made some predictions about the presence and growth of women and persons of color by the year 2000, a year that has now come and gone:

- Women will account for more than 47% of the total work force and 61% of all American women will be employed.

- African Americans will make up 12% of the total labor force, with Hispanics at 10% and Asians at 4%.

- The numbers of American workers in the 35-54 age group will increase by more than 25 million–from 38% of the work force in 1985 to 51%. The 16-24 worker age group will decline by almost 2 million, or 8%.

With that strategy, we made progress. By 1994, GM could announce that every vehicle built and sold in the United States had components that were produced by minority-owned companies. Every single car and truck! We could announce an increase in the number of minority dealers, who generated more than $3.8 billion in sales and sold nearly 260,000 new and used vehicles. Dealer diversity was important, because it meant we were empowering ownership and decision-making. That's where the power is.

In the financial realm, we could announce that we had deposited more than $1 billion in accounts with minority-owned banks–and that we did business with virtually every minority-owned bank in the country. We could announce that more than $13 billion of our property damage insurance was managed by minority-owned insurance brokers. And we could announce that our venture capital firm, Motor Enterprises–an entity specifically formed to make start-up and expansion capital available to minority-owned firms–had been able to leverage about $100 million in capital for such businesses through seed loans and investments.

In 1994, I was promoted from Truck Operations to Vice-President of Corporate Affairs. With the theory in place, I made what some would call a radical move. It was a move that would upset the apple cart, not only within GM, but throughout Detroit's grassroots community. I ended up having to explain my actions to some of the city's most prominent activists.

I made a decision to essentially abolish the Urban Affairs Department at GM. Urban Affairs departments had become a "ghetto" of sorts in corporate America, and everyone knew it. It was the place where corporations parked their diversity efforts. And too often, that's precisely what happened: diversity efforts parked there, and never moved.

It was my feeling that this would have to change. I didn't see simply "improving" the department; I felt the ghetto had to be razed. After all, this was the department that monitored the "set-aside" program. I am for affirmative action, but dead-set against set-asides. Why give African American and other minority businesses part of the pie, when they should by rights have access to the whole pie? I wanted more than a sliver for these companies. I knew that many of them could compete on their own terms well beyond that which the set-aside would provide.

The community didn't see it that way. In fact, one of my employees contacted the NAACP about planning a major demonstration in front of GM's headquarters on West Grand Boulevard to protest the action.

I found myself meeting with NAACP President Wendell Anthony, Pastor of Fellowship Chapel. President Anthony and I had a long talk, and I explained what I was doing and why. He didn't agree with the march, and we've been friends ever since.

The automobile industry has evolved in some very interesting ways. Now, it is creating dynasties led and peopled by persons of color-and for the first time allowing people of color to move into the top executive ranks. I was glad to have been a part of this not-so-quiet, but decidedly non-violent, revolution.

Chapter 5

How to Beat the System: A Message to Young and Old

I have worked all my life to "beat the system." And what I mean by that is this: I have worked to secure roles, responsibilities, and opportunities that allowed me to have decision-making power to affect lives in a profound and significant way.

I was a corporate citizen. But as a corporate citizen, I found a way to introduce diversity into what was once the largest corporation in the world: General Motors. I found a way to create opportunity for African American entrepreneurs through the creation of the Clark Technology Park. I found a way to introduce the concept of diversity as a "business imperative," the only way to conduct business in a global economy and society. In fact, not long after I drafted GM's Diversity Statement, I looked up to find that Texaco, embroiled in its own controversy over corporate culture and racism, had pretty much lifted their statement verbatim from our own.

And I was blessed with the opportunity to help create, from scratch, one of the first institutes to formally and systematically address racism within the U.S. Armed Forces–or any other institution: the Race Relations Institute.

How can more of us move into these kinds of positions? Even more importantly, how can those of us currently in those kinds of positions move to create needed change for our nation and world?

I was fortunate. I grew up in an environment that included blacks and whites living (somewhat) together. Most African Americans have not had that experience. Most of us grow up in predominately African American, urban communities. We live in African American neighborhoods and go to African American schools. Our social and cultural reactions are formed by that environment.

That is a problem; it is also an opportunity. The main problem is socialization. When we move into the corporate world, a second lens is layered onto our original viewpoint. We're in a different world, and so new experiences create confusion in our perception. We're not sure that we're seeing things as they really are.

The corporate culture doesn't help. Traditional organizations keep us confused by reacting schizophrenically to us-gladly acknowledging our presence on the one hand, but not accepting us as "one of the boys (or girls)" on the other. This plays out in heightened scrutiny and criticism of our work, in missed opportunities, and in an absence of effective mentors. As a result, we have a "we-they" relationship with corporate America: we see "them" as a powerful enemy to be overcome.

But what if we considered a different reality? In truth, the Anglo corporate structure and the African American community are two powerful, discrete entities in the United States that have often engaged in profound ideological conflict. Our increasing presence in corporate America has forced the issue on many fronts–for the better, I might add.

And this has happened because some very shrewd individuals have been able to work on two fronts: individual achievement, which is necessary to even get a place "at the table" in corporate America, especially for African Americans; and collective progress, which can only happen when individuals work in strategic ways to foster change.

I think back to Mrs. Rosa Parks and her statement to me years ago: "Mr. Brooks, make sure you always work to enable other blacks to get where you are." I have never forgotten that statement, and I never will. To those African Americans in influential positions throughout corporate America, I say to you: you will never know the impact that your words of wisdom will have on an individual. Choose words that encourage, but also words that challenge those coming behind you.

I make this next point carefully, and ask you to think along with me. As more corporations embrace diversity (even those who embrace it warily and tentatively), we find that more employees are being empowered to act in ways that improve these companies' bottom line results. I would suggest that part of that empowerment for us as African Americans is not using racism as a crutch.

Not that racism does not exist. A poll suggested that 95% of African American business people thought their career advancement had been hindered because of race. I'm sure that statistic is consistent with what you know and have experienced.

But none of us can afford to trot that out every time we experience a setback. Performance is the point, not racism. That is a hard reality–but it is very real, especially to those who have bumped up against it.

So, how to beat the system? First, perform. Then, be a participant. Then, look for strategic ways to make change wherever you have an influence. To do that, you will have to look for the informal system that exists within every corporation. That's the network of who you know, the cliques, the old networks that are perpetuated with every generation of new employees. Some managers, even some black managers, will try to tell you it doesn't exist. Don't believe them. They're either naive, don't want you to play, or haven't been invited to the party themselves.

You will have to make sure that you have an "ol' boy" or "ol' girl" network of your own. It is that back-channel communications system that will be one of your most important assets. It will warn you early of developments that may affect you, and serve as a basis for long-term friendships within your organization. As you develop this network, it will be helpful for you to build up a "favor bank." Anything you do something to help someone in a pinch gets put into that bank and allows you to access resources of value when it is time for you to make your move.

The people in your network should definitely include some of those in your "observation gallery." That is the universe of people who are watching you. They may be superiors, or peers, or even subordinates. Whoever they are, you must make it your business to know who is observing your behavior–and how they can impact your progress or your plans.

Then: make sure you know how to "manage" your boss. Your success is almost always dependent upon the success of the people placed over you. Make your boss look good, and you will be able to do things that others cannot. Make your boss look good, and who knows? They just might move out of your way!

Once you have some individual achievements in your reputation bank, you can then work towards the change you have in mind. Here, I urge you to remember one thing: it is much easier to change behavior than change attitudes. The person who works to change attitudes is constantly beating his head against the wall.

I never took that road. Whenever I worked to create change in an organization, I always emphasized that the goal was for certain behaviors to change. The teams I led or in which I participated drove home the message that we were specifically not trying to change hearts. We simply demanded–and backed up our demands with actions and consequences understood by all–that the employee perform, or not perform, very concrete and defined actions. Of course, we backed up our insistence with education to dispel ethnic and racial myths and introduce the practical advantages of diversity.

And ironically, we found that these "baby step" behavioral changes sometimes resulted in changed, revamped opinions. It didn't always happen, but it certainly was more effective than going the other route.

Most importantly, LEARN HOW TO LEARN. After you have

long completed your formal education, you must continue to read and to study. Job categories are changing at a breathtaking pace, faster than any other time in history. Many of the occupations that will exist in the next 50 years don't even exist today.

It is possible to "beat the system." It takes work, strategy, a commitment to excellence, and a refusal to back down. It takes knowing where the power is in an organization–and seeking to move into those positions. Most importantly, it takes collaboration; finding someone who is as passionate as you about change and learning how to leverage a team to make that change. And the great thing is, you can apply the rules of change in businesses, governments, community organizations, churches–any institution that is seeking to better itself or its surrounding community.

Especially to Young Adults: Brooks's "Ten Commandments for Success"

Thou shalt know thy culture. Find out your heritage and celebrate it.
One of my great joys was teaching African American heritage and culture to U.S. military personnel. I was able to affect some of the most racist people I have ever come across. But the groundwork had already been laid. I knew my history. I knew what had to be taught.

Thou shalt follow through on your commitments. Be reliable and dependable.
In some of my first professional positions, I went the distance to make sure that I did all that was required. I did everything I could to make sure that my work was above reproach. I knew what I was up against, and I did not ever want to give my superiors a reason to criticize. That is what allowed me to move up the ladder to positions of even greater influence.

Thou shalt be a team player. Work well with others.
There are very few things that you can effectively accomplish alone. The best team players are upbeat and confi-

dent. They're not known as complainers. They don't mind "getting their hands dirty." No job is "beneath" them. They are focused, simply, on making sure the job gets done.

Thou shalt not burn bridges unless you know how to walk on water.

I think about some of my "valley" experiences. Even with the most impossible people, I tried to maintain a positive attitude. My strategy was to let the truth speak for itself, without getting into personal vendettas and attacks. It worked well; some of my worst enemies actually became my greatest supporters.

Thou shalt talk smart–but listen first.

Your grandmother probably told you this: "that's why you have two ears and one mouth." But it's true, ageless advice. If you fail to listen, you put yourself at risk–of having the right answers to the wrong questions! Always try to repeat what you think the person is saying in your own words. That convinces them that you hear them, and that your response will be genuine and address their concerns.

Thou shalt not give up or say "I can't." Be persistent and courageous.

I think back to the time we put together the Clark Street Technology Park. No one at the time thought it would work. A technology park filled with viable minority businesses? How would we amass the capital to acquire and prepare the land? How could we afford to address the environmental concerns and meet the stringent regulations? And what minority firms were prosperous enough to make a go of the project? We worked to answer those questions, one by one. We did our homework. I had been fortunate enough to see minority companies up close–companies who I knew had great potential for long-term success. Companies that others may not have believed in as much. Now, Clark Street Technology Park boasts companies that employ hundreds of people and contribute millions of dollars to the local economy.

Thou shalt continue to learn...and learn "how to learn." Getting an education is an everyday thing.
Did you know that every time you learn something, you develop more connections in your brain? The more connections, the more you feed your ability and your intelligence. There are scientists that say that multiple connections can even protect against the "old age" diseases of senility and Alzheimer's. Never stop learning!

Thou shalt keep thy personal life "personal." The workplace is not a social event to discuss or arrange your private life.
I have found this to be one of the most violated "commandments." I have seen enough scandals (you probably have too, in the news, which has become more gossipy than ever) to understand that you really can't trust anyone to keep a secret about your personal life. Many lives have been shipwrecked because they told something "in secret" to someone who told someone else "in secret," who told someone else, until it reached the wrong ears. Keep it on a professional level at all times; you'll avoid much heartache and stress!

Thou shalt tell people your professional aspirations
And while you're doing that, make sure you explain how you qualify for them. It's okay to aspire to greater things. But don't expect people to read your mind, and don't hide your light under a bushel.

Thou shalt remember that the company you work for has one purpose: to make money. No money, no paycheck. And money is made with the help of productive and effective workers.
Even when I was making the case for diversity at General Motors, I kept things bottom-line oriented. I was one of the first to make a "business case" for diversity. I linked diversity to the changing national and global marketplace, to the rise in buying power of African Americans and other groups. I had experts and statistics to back me up. That is how you will have to approach change anywhere; you will have to show what's in it for

them, as well as for those you are trying to impact.

You CAN beat the system. If you don't believe it, go back and read this book all over again!